Write to Riches

7 Practical Steps to Manifesting Abundance from Your Books

Renee Rose

WRITE2RICHES

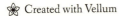

To Lee Savino, who has been my partner in crime on this author abundance journey since the day we met and was infinitely gracious when I pitched her on co-writing this book with me and then reversed directions and decided I wanted to write it on my own.
I love you!

Want Author Affirmations Sent to Your Inbox?

Author Abundance Affirmations

Sign up to receive a weekly Millionaire Author Affirmation delivered straight from the Universe (via me) to your inbox! These weekly reminders will keep you on track and positive as you become your Millionaire Author self. https://www.subscribepage.com/authorabundanceaffirmations

Chapter 1

Introduction

Cha-ching!

December 2020, eight years after I published my first romance and launched my author career, I finally heard the *cha-ching* sound on BookReport heralding my first official seven-figure year as an author. I'd earned one million dollars in royalties—a dream come true!

My "overnight success" had finally struck. I'd literally been dream-boarding this goal since that first book, and my ship had finally arrived. To celebrate, I cut into a gourmet cake, uncorked a bottle of wine, and lit sparklers with my kids, dancing around my kitchen with a giddy sense of accomplishment.

My system had finally paid off. I followed the steps and found more and more return on the investment in transforming my mindset. Now, I'm sharing the seven practical steps with you.

I want to start by saying that you are amazing.

You are already a success. You wrote a book! Maybe an entire catalog of books. That's more than most people ever dream of.

But I get it—you want it all. You want to be a six or seven (or eight!) figure author. You want to buy that new car, put your kid through college, retire your spouse. You want total fandemonium—raving fans desperate for your next book. Lining up at the next book con to get to your table. If you're like me, you're dreaming of seeing your work on the big screen or television.

You want it all.

So do I!

And why shouldn't you have it?

Chances are good, I've been exactly where you are. You're an author. Maybe you've written one book, maybe you've written one hundred, but you still have big dreams and despite doing all the things, you haven't hit them yet. You know what's possible. You witnessed the meteoric success of *Fifty Shades of Grey* and the more moderate successes of author friends and colleagues.

Maybe you've had a taste of success yourself, but then you plateaued. Whether you've made three, four, five, or six figures a year as an author, you want more. You play the comparison game, and sometimes it leaves you feeling flat and defeated.

You're doing everything you're supposed to to succeed in this field.

You work hard. You're slogging away. You have your butt in your chair every day, writing all the words. You use your social media every way you know how. You're networking, marketing, advertising. But despite shoveling coal on the fire to keep the dream alive, your ship hasn't come in yet. Or it has, but you want more.

This book is for you.

Being an authorpreneur is a tough gig. It's a solitary

career, so we often feel alone. There can be a strong sense of competition for what you may perceive as only a few prime spots in the sun. Defeating thoughts can creep in. Imposter syndrome. Fears that your books aren't good enough, or that you don't know how to sell them properly. It's easy to feel like if you just had one crucial piece of information, you could put it all together.

You're not alone if you function from a sense of hunger and striving that hints of desperation, as well as the constant fear of failure. You watch others hit number one in the Amazon store or on the *USA Today* list and wonder, "Why not me?" or you think, "I'll never get there." You hear about how they did it, and you say, "They got lucky, they got in before the ebook/audio/Facebook ad boom," or you think "That method doesn't work for me."

Being any kind of artist can be painful. Your books are your babies, and you want them to succeed. Maybe you've put a time limit on your dream. Like, "if I can't pay the bills with these books by the end of the year, I'll quit writing."

Please don't quit. I have your back.

The *Write to Riches* method will take the pain out of being an author. If you follow the steps in this book, the abundance will start to flow. You'll clear that sense of failure or imposter's syndrome, along with your money wounds and blocks to abundance, which hold you back from having the author career you want right now. You'll step into your own power as an artist and a creative, find confidence in your books, and know the pathways to promote them.

In short, you'll learn what I did, step by step, to go from working a nine dollar an hour job to becoming a million-aire author—and how you can, too.

Do you want to:

- Attract raving fans
- Have your books go viral
- Hit bestseller lists
- Feel inspired and love both your books and your process
- Create wealth beyond what you've imagined from your books?

Before I started feeling abundant, I experienced flashes of success, but I didn't get consistent results. I chased success from a position of lack. If you've subscribed at all to the Law of Attraction or as some prefer, the Law of Assumption, you know your thoughts create your reality. So my desperation for success (and my fear I was going to fail) became a match for not having consistent success and being plagued with the idea that I wasn't good enough.

The answer to this dilemma is to work harder.

Just kidding!

That is what I thought. It was what had been trained into me by my hard-working, raised-on-a-farm mom, right along with the belief that I wasn't enough and only humility, good deeds, and pinching pennies would make me so (all energies I had to work to clear to be able to receive abundance).

No, the answer lies in an abundance mindset, which is more than practicing gratitude or the loveable Ted Lasso approach to positivity. (But I seriously love that show with my whole heart.)

I'm not saying gratitude and positivity don't work or aren't a part of it, but if you're not feeling that mindset, it can seem hokey and put-on. Like repeating affirmations you don't believe. This book will go to the core of your issues and give you the power to release them, tap into your own genius, and call in your future life now.

The *Write to Riches* method is a seven-step process to create abundance. It doesn't just work for authors. This process could be used to manifest anything in your life, but since I am an author, I've put it to use for this purpose.

The *Write to Riches* method will help you to transform your mindset, re-program your energy and abundance to receiving mode, and drink in the pleasure of writing again.

It's an in-depth practice of all the facets involved in manifesting your dream career, beginning with clearing limiting beliefs, getting clear on your intentions, and ending with trust and receiving.

Spoiler alert: I don't have the answers for you.

You do. You already know all the things, and when you don't, you'll attract the information easily when you need it.

You won't be copying my journey to success because we each have our own genius, our own pathways. Part of the *Write to Riches* method will be training you to tap into your own knowing, your own intuition or awareness, to create your highest future.

This book is not to explain how I got to seven figures as an author, except from a mindset point of view. The steps I took won't be the steps you'll take to achieve your success. Abundance won't happen for you the same way—or maybe it will. I'm not going to share the latest tips and tricks in the industry—how to craft better TikTok videos or optimize your Bookbub ads because whether you're already all over that stuff or have never heard of it, you should know that what works today for me won't work in three months or however long has passed before you pick up this book. Rather, this playbook is designed to lay out the seven practical steps to magnetize abundance to your author career and manifest your dreams.

There are lots of books out there that give this same information from a more scientific or psychological viewpoint with studies to back up all the theories. I'm not a scientist: I'm a creative. I follow my gut in writing and marketing my books. My language is energy—that's what I use to create my business, books, and future. However, this is not all woo-woo. This book contains a multitude of practical tools for you, as an author, to apply, including exercises to help you access your own intuition to create the future you've been dreaming of.

This is a work/play book. I suggest you return to this book again and again—every time you're ready to bring your career to the next level.

I have many resources available to support your progress through *Write to Riches*. I would love for you to join the Author Abundance Facebook group and post any revelations you have while working through this book. It's a wonderful, supportive group of authors who will cheer on your wins and celebrate with you as you open to your abundance. I also have meditations available as a bonus to this book, and for deeper support or faster change, consider joining the Author Abundance monthly membership group, featuring monthly video calls to answer questions, clear energy and provide support as well as a library of meditations.

My Background

Twenty-some years ago, before the movie *The Secret* came out teaching that our intentions and thoughts create our reality, I had a neighbor who subscribed to this interesting belief that if you just "put out there" to the Universe[1] the thing you wanted, the Universe would respond.

That easily.

After witnessing her make miracles happen in her life very quickly, I followed my neighbor's example. I "put it out there" that I'd like to own a house, even though I worked a nine dollar an hour job, had no savings, and had lived in five places in the past two years—something I discovered mortgage companies frowned on. I also "put it out there" that I'd like a job that actually used my college degree in English/Creative Writing but still allowed me a flexible schedule to dance professionally, to replace the part-time secretarial work I'd picked up to maintain flexibility for rehearsals.

Within weeks, my dad, out of the blue and without knowing the intentions I'd made, asked if I'd be interested in his help investing in—you guessed it—a house. A few weeks after that, a friend in my dance company told me there was an opening for a technical writer at an engineering firm, and believe it or not, in a time long before flexible work arrangements—they were willing to have me work only 30 hours a week to accommodate my rehearsal schedule. The job came with a raise and a great benefit package.

Boom.

I was forever hooked on the magic of manifesting.

Years later, after a friend gave me a Jennifer Crusie novel, I fell in love with romance. In my college creative writing program, we were taught that only literary fiction was worth reading and writing, so consequently, I'd looked down my nose at genre fiction. But the happily-ever-afters of romance spoke to my Law-of-Attraction loving heart. Why read the "life sucks but I learned something" of literary fiction when I could read something that feels good? Wouldn't I want to vibe in the happy, not the sad?

I started reading romance and spent a year writing an epically long medieval romance that has never seen the light of day. But the Universe had my back. Another friend mentioned this phenomenon called *Fifty Shades of Grey* that was changing the reading and writing world, and I heard the angels bugling. Kinky power dynamics in romance *was my jam*. When I realized there was a market for it, I sat down and penned a 25,000 word story in six days and sent it off to a kinky niche publisher. As luck (or quantum entanglements) would have it, they had a new editor on the job, and my book was the first on his desk. Two weeks later, the book was published, and because it was 2012 and the early days of ebooks, the little book went up on Amazon and sold. My first check was $4800—enough to pay my mortgage.

It felt like a message from the Universe. I'd found my calling. I could use my degree—and my fantasies—to make a living.

Of course, not everything went as smoothly from there. As I'm sure you know, what works in this business now will change in three months. My next few books had *meh* results, but I kept at it. I had a few years of churning out the books and making forty to fifty thousand a year, which was a decent living, considering 90 percent of authors never hit five figures a year, but I had much bigger dreams.

I also had struggles. Doubts. Reinventions. I persevered.

I learned to follow the trends and write to market. I

tried the rapid-release method on Kindle Unlimited in 2017, and I went from making fifty thousand a year to two hundred and fifty thousand.

As my backlist grew, so did my income. Using Facebook ads, I was able to double that income the following year, but then as every other author also learned how to use Facebook ads, I plateaued again, going from half a million dollars in 2018 to six hundred and fifty thousand dollars in 2019 with much higher ad expenses.

In 2020, I went wide and released translations of my work in German, French, Italian, and Spanish, which brought me to my seven-figure goal—the one I'd been dreaming of from the beginning. The one that seemed like pie in the sky back then. The next year, I doubled that again as my translation backlist grew.

Did I work my butt off?

Yes.

You could say I made it through perseverance and hard work, but that's a mindset I've been working on busting out of (because what if we could create all our dreams with total ease?). I certainly had my nose to the grindstone for all those years. I worked hard, wrote a lot of books, and invested in marketing. I studied all the "how-to's".

But I don't attribute my success to rapid-releasing, writing to market, Facebook ads, or chasing trends, even though those were key for me. I attribute it to healing my money wounds, calling in the abundance, following my gut, opening up to receive. I credit my success to the power of intention and manifestation. To drinking my coffee every morning from my Millionaire Author mug and clearing negative self-talk. To releasing self-judgment and limiting beliefs and acknowledging my strengths. To holding that unwavering belief that I would one day be a millionaire author. I used the *Write to Riches* method to see opportunities and trust myself to choose what would work for me and what wouldn't. Basically, the steps I will teach you in this book.

So grab a pen, make a cup of tea or coffee, find a comfy chair, and let's dive in!

Step 1: Clear the Deck

Chapter 2

Addressing your Money Wounds and Clearing Limiting Beliefs

T he first step to manifesting anything is to clear out the limiting beliefs and heal your wounds. You can't create the future you desire if you don't believe you're worthy or that it's possible.

I'm guessing if you picked up this book, you've already boarded the law of attraction train. If not, the basic premise is that our thoughts create our reality. The energy we dwell in is the energy we attract. If you spend your time thinking about, talking about, and energizing lack in your career–lack of royalties, lack of readers, lack of good reviews, lack of any kind–that is what will keep showing up for you.

The first step to healing the pain in your author career is to identify, address, and clear all the thoughts that hold your current reality in place. On the surface, you may not think you have any—or just a few big ones—but the truth is even if you're already living your dream life, there's always more to clear. It's a continuous process, like the peeling of an onion.

We tend to make ourselves so small! We have a million limiting beliefs that stop us all day every day. Most of them are like those background programs running on a computer.

We don't even notice, we just operate from them like they're truths instead of lies we've bought to keep ourselves from greatness.

This stuff sits in your energetic field and drags it down. It becomes a negative influencing field. It's not you, but it may feel that way. The real you—your core self, your infinite being self—doesn't function from pain or limitation.

You can have whatever you want. Bestselling books, a full time author career, millions of readers all over the world who passionately love your books. The only one stopping you from creating your future is you. More specifically, your limiting beliefs.

The truth is, everything you want is available to you. Yes, this includes money. The reason you don't have what you want is because you've been pushing it away. I've been there. The reason we push money away is because, on some level, we perceive it as a threat or wrong, maybe even bad, complicated, too different from what we are, not the truth of us, a change agent, or we're not worthy or "enough".

What if people don't like my book? What if I get one-star reviews? What if they call me a hack? Maybe I'm not a real author? Maybe I'm an imposter?

Sound familiar? The doubts may not be as obvious as that, though. Even if you don't think those actual thoughts consciously, the underlying energy is there.

We tell ourselves all kinds of stories that destroy our chances at success. Things like, "I'm not as good as _____ (insert favorite writer), and I never will be."

"This release didn't go as well as the last one. Maybe readers don't like _____ anymore."

Or have you ever heard someone say: "I tried having a newsletter, and it didn't work for me." or "I tried Facebook ads, and they don't work for me"? How about, "Bookbub hates me. They'll never give me a deal." Or this one, "I've tried everything, but I don't know what else I can possibly do."

Have you ever had these thoughts yourself?

The first step is to start noticing what your thoughts reveal if you have the courage to listen.

Any time you feel anything other than light and fluffy about anything at all, lean in and ask, *what lie am I believing?*

Because our natural state—the state of our infinite being self—is joy. Expansion. Abundance. Gratitude. So if you're feeling anything less than that, you've bought into a lie.

In this step, we're going to excavate and clear all the lies you harbor around your creative process, writing and marketing your books, and money. All lies about abundance.

Clearing the deck before you start creating is essential.

Before I truly dug into this step, I want to admit something. When I first worked with it, I used the law of attraction to ignore the fears or feelings I didn't like. I tried to change what I feared by covering them up, disguising them, layering what I wanted over the top.

I felt like a shitty writer? I'd turn away from the anxiety that feeling brought up and firmly place a new affirmation in front of it. There were things in my marriage that weren't working, but instead of really digging in and addressing them, I hid my head in the sand, hoping and wishing, and trying to manifest them away. I thought I could outcreate my fears.

You can manifest this way. It still sometimes works. For example, I could manifest my husband bringing me home flowers after a fight because I visualized it, but he didn't want to bring me the flowers, neither of us felt satisfied, and the gift I created didn't solve the underlying issue.

This process of trying to out-create my fears and emotions led to mixed success in my author business and in my life. Sometimes it worked to manifest what I wanted, and sometimes it didn't. But the underlying anxiety—the fears that I wasn't enough, that I'd never succeed, that I didn't fit in—those didn't go away. The pain was still there beneath it. I was still creating from a frantic, I'll-never-get-there energy.

Do you ever find yourself feeling the same?

Clearing your Core Wounds

If you write fiction, you're probably experienced at identifying your characters' core wounds. It's their most limiting thought that keeps them from having what they truly desire. Once you know their core wound, writing their arc becomes easy. In romance, it's what makes characters resist love and refuse it altogether at the black moment. The happily-ever-after can't come until they've addressed it and actively, courageously chosen beyond it.

We have to change to have our own happily-ever-afters. If you don't identify your core wounds, you can't address them. You can't recognize them as the culprits when your mindset slides down into the pit of despair.

For me, my core wounds are not being enough, fear of abandonment, and not fitting in. That's why I write romance featuring possessive males like werewolves, aliens, or mafia men who fiercely and utterly claim their female for life. She's always enough—in fact, all he needs—and he won't ever let her go (*swoon*).

USA Today Bestselling author Lyz Kelley was the one who helped me crystalize this as a strength in my writing. She coaches authors on creating their taglines based on their core wounds and what they're trying to solve, so she helped me find my tagline: "Claimed by Love."

But I can't wait for a dominant werewolf to come claim me in order to heal my wounds. I have to believe I *am* enough. To know I have my own back and won't ever abandon myself. To see that I do belong anywhere I want to be. There's a place for me at the table of bestselling authors.

I recognize I have a tendency to go into victim mode (still hoping a dominant hero will swoop in and rescue me) and to play pathetic. None of these energies create the future I want. Instead, I have to notice when those energies arise and make the conscious choice not to function from them, to clear them, and to come from a place of clear choice and power.

As I mentioned before, a deep-seated lie I often buy into is "I'm not good enough". It's part of what made me work so hard to make a million dollars. I was trying to prove, prove, prove that I might be good enough. Again, notice the whiff of desperation behind that endeavor.

What if I just decided I was good enough? I wouldn't stop creating, but it would be with so much more joy instead of angsty necessity.

There have been many points in my life where I knew exactly what it would take to be successful at a given thing, but because my self-image didn't match, I refused to take the steps that I could see clearly laid out for me. I wasn't sure if I was worthy. Whether I'd be able to handle that up-level.

I started out writing erotica, and I brought shame to my self-image as a writer. I wasn't a "real" writer. I wasn't "mainstream". I didn't think there was a place for me at the table with the real authors. I went to my first RWA meetings afraid they'd scorn me and what I wrote (thankfully, that didn't happen–or it never reached me if it did).

My self-image grew over time, but it took conscious effort. It still takes conscious effort! A few years ago, my co-author Lee Savino and I figured out how to get our books translated and marketed in Germany. Knowing other authors struggled with it and that it was a great revenue possibility, we set up a small translation house and started getting other authors' work out there. But my self-image was still of the struggling author–the *I have to do everything myself and there aren't enough hours in the day* author, not a business entrepreneur who can hire competent people and oversee everything in a few hours a week. When I confessed my struggles and need to slow down before I melted down to my business coach, he suggested we hire a full-time German editor to oversee the whole program, work with the translators, and streamline. He said,

"Now is the time to hit the gas, not the brakes."

I didn't take his advice, even though I knew then and I know now that it was sound. My self-image just couldn't expand quickly enough to see myself running a publishing empire yet. I still felt I had to do everything myself, and I couldn't focus on it all.

We hit the brakes. It's been almost two years, and we're just now starting to consider firing it up again. Now, I am better at supporting myself with a virtual assistant and seeing myself as the business manager, not the person who has to do every task herself.

I don't see these challenges as a failure. I'm not judging myself for it. I've learned over the years to have compassion and accept myself where I am. But it's so painfully obvious to me that had I followed those steps and allowed myself to become a queen bee of business, it would have easily succeeded instead of limping along.

I had a similar faltering when it came to stepping into public speaking as an abundance mindset author coach. So much anxiety came up–who did I think I was? What if I failed? Am I *really worthy* of wearing that mantle?

I'm still working through those doubts, but the point is, I'm aware of them. They're not buried in my subconscious running the show anymore. I am dragging them out to be examined and discarded.

I am also done with other lies, judgments, and excuses I use, including:

"I'm not good at networking."

"I have to make everyone happy."

"I'm socially awkward."

"My books aren't deep enough / well-written enough."

"I'm disorganized."

"The sales / readers could all dry up tomorrow."

"I'm not ready" (for all kinds of things).

I'm realizing all of those self-judgments might actually be barriers I put in place to hide my greatest strengths from myself. It was like giving myself a handicap when I came into this lifetime, so I wouldn't surpass everyone around me with my greatness. If I would clear them, I might find those areas are all areas I actually have a special capacity, not a deficiency.

Other ways we limit ourselves include procrastination,

fear, doubt, regret, shame, blame. Going into victim mode. Making yourself pathetic, making yourself small to fit in with others.

Even having done a lot of deep work, I still have to constantly clear limiting beliefs. Recently, the main water line to the house broke, and I had a lake in front of my house. It shouldn't be a big problem. I now have money to fix things, so that financial anxiety didn't kick in. Yet, I found the old energies of making myself small with home repairs (because my ex used to handle all that) rearing their heads. I questioned myself. I second-guessed who to call. How to handle it. Replace the whole line or just the leak? Could I trust my maintenance guy, or did I need to get three quotes? I'll bet nothing about that situation sounds daunting to you, and yet for some reason, it was to me. Because it was heaped under a pile of "I can't do this" and "I don't know what I'm doing" and "I can't trust my own judgment".

Fortunately, I have the tools to move through these situations. The first step was to notice the thoughts and beliefs. I knew better than to call a friend and complain about the situation–my old *modus operandi* when something in my life went wrong. That's just marinating in the energy I don't want. Instead, I dug into why it was so stressful to me and unearthed the beliefs that I didn't trust myself in this situation.

I cleared that belief (we'll talk more about how to clear later in this section) and used my intuition to make a choice between contractors. I instantly felt lighter and stopped second-guessing myself. A couple days later, when I still hadn't heard from the contractor who I'd picked, my gut said to change the plan. Instead of going into thoughts like, wow I made the wrong choice, it's true I really don't know what I'm doing, I acknowledged that energy changes. I may not be privy to the whole picture. Maybe that contractor had his own emergency and is no longer the perfect person. Who knows? I trusted my gut. The other contractor came and was wonderfully helpful.

Obviously this isn't a home repair book, but our mindset affects the way we feel in every moment. Any time you're not feeling expansive, free, abundance, ease, you can pull out these tools to create a new reality for yourself.

So your task for this step is to use the writing prompts that follow to start identifying all of your limiting beliefs, blocks, wounds. Make a list. If you're willing, share what you discover in the Facebook group because your insights will help others. Then choose today to let them all go. At the end of this step, I've provided a number of tools to choose from to clear and heal those wounds, so you can start fresh and invite abundance in.

The following are common thought patterns that inhibit us from doing what we are here on this Earth to do, *which is to shine*. Are any of them painfully familiar to you?

- I will never succeed.
- Blaming others: _____[Amazon, Bookbub, FB, another author] screwed me over.
- I make unforgivable mistakes.
- I have no confidence.
- Fear thinking: I can't trust anyone.
- Victim thinking: This always happens to me.
- All or nothing thinking: It has to be done this way or it won't work.
- I am a bad person.
- Should statements: I should ____ [write 5,000 words a day, publish every month, send out my newsletter, and ___].

- Lack statements: I would do better if only
  _____.
- I am not worthy / I am more worthy than others.
- Magnification statements: Facebook shut down my ad account, so my writing career is over.
- Minimization statements: I don't need an editor. I just read my books out loud. That's good enough.
- Personalizing: Bookbub hates me.
- Catastrophizing: My last launch failed, my career is over.
- Overgeneralization: Fantasy isn't selling. Newsletters don't work. Facebook is off.
- I am a failure / I am better than everyone.

Freewriting: Tap into Your Genius

Please grab your workbook or get out your journal. When you approach the journal contemplations, treat them like you would a freewriting exercise. Keep your pen moving across the page and shut off the internal editor. Don't think—just write. You're going to tap into your subconscious or intuition to get the answers that will truly contribute to your abundance and the future you're trying to create. You're contemplating in writing–everything is unpacking–every thought, every impulse, every feeling, every picture that comes to you. Allow it all. Begin with the first thing that comes to mind. Don't try to get the right answer or to answer from your cognitive brain —conclusions limit possibilities. Instead, really use your perception and awareness to access your contemplations and allow them space on the page and in your consciousness.

Remember—keep the pen moving across the page. This is the place of allowing, of freedom, of courage. This isn't the place to edit. Allow the ideas to flow, so you can tap into your subconscious and really dig into the intuitive answers that will bring you maximum insight. The more you allow yourself to play with your contemplations, the faster you can clear all your blocks to abundance. Are you willing to surprise yourself?

Write until nothing more comes out, then move onto the next one. If you get tired or feel exhausted, take a break and come back to it later. This isn't a race. You're moving to a life in which you truly embody and live abundance. Where riches are your easy norm. When you truly allow yourself to fully explore, it can be a lot for your nervous system to absorb. You're bringing the anti-consciousness– the knowledge you are resisting in your life–into consciousness. There are things we stick our heads in the sand about– this will uncover them. Your entire construct of reality may shatter and fall, and that's okay. That's what we want. After all, what are you letting go of? Lack. Limits. Beliefs that trap you. You have to be willing to leave behind the old to become the new. Are you ready to learn something new about yourself? Are you ready to truly explore? To see everything?

Let's unearth the possible core wounds you function from. Don't think. Just write everything that comes to you, even if it's not a whole thought:

1. I can't be a millionaire author because
   _____.
2. The lies I'm believing that keep me from being my biggest, brightest self are_____.
3. I've been telling myself this lie since_____?

4. The fear or anxiety that makes me stop myself comes from _____.
5. I block myself from being the brilliant millionaire author that I am in these ways _____ .

Are you waiting for someone else to discover you? To give you permission? What are the things you believe must happen before you can go to the next level? Answer the next question with the steps you think have to happen first: (hint, they may not be true. You're just using them as excuses for not having your future life now).

1. I will be a successful author when _____ .
2. My biggest fear about success is_____ .
3. My biggest fear about failure is_____.
4. I distract myself from becoming my future self by _____.
5. My excuses for why I can't move forward yet are _____.

The great thing about these contemplations is that you can return to them. You might be willing to allow some aspect of a belief into your consciousness, and later, when you contemplate again, something else emerges. Clearing limiting beliefs is not a one-and-done process. With each layer of the onion we allow ourselves to pull back, we get to the truth of who we are, and from that expanded place, we can dive in again and again, continually receiving.

Chapter 3

How to Clear the Crud

Congratulations! You just generated a lot of great thoughts, beliefs, and patterns that can be cleared, so you can go to the next level. As quickly as you identify blocks and resistance, you can let it all go.

Go to your journal or workbook and circle the biggest blocks or core wounds that came up for you. Now pick one to work with. I suggest you follow what feels light for you—you may want to start with your biggest, deepest wound, or you may want to pick an easy one to begin with. There is no right way to do this, except what feels good to you.

The very act of discovery—of freewriting to reveal where you're blocked—brings the thoughts and beliefs out of the anti-conscious or subconscious and into your awareness. That alone begins the healing, but to support your shift into a mindset, let's clear it completely from your energetic field.

Name the wound or limiting belief you're working on. For the sake of explanation, I'm going to pick one like, "I can't be a millionaire author because my books aren't good enough."

First of all–notice that this is a lie. If you use your emotions or your reaction to it as a guide, anything that doesn't make you feel good is a lie. Therefore, the statement can't be true. Are you with me?

You don't actually have to do anything beyond simply choosing to change it. If you believe you need more than choice, there are many powerful clearing methods out there.

It could be as simple as writing down the belief on a piece of paper and burning it. It doesn't have to be magic or mysterious.

You could also track the root of that belief by asking why.

Why do I believe that my books aren't good enough?

Why do I believe that?

Why do I believe that?

On and on until you trace the place where the belief that you aren't good enough began. Then acknowledge the lie of all lies–the lies that birthed that belief.

Now that you've uncovered a lie, let's create something different:

1. **Make a Choice**

Are you going to keep functioning from that lie? Or are you ready to rocket out of this pattern and have the future you've been pining for? If you're not ready to choose out of it, by all means, dig a hole and sit in it. Play pathetic and wait for someone to come and fix things for you–I'm sure that will work eventually. Or find the people in your life who will sit with you in that hole. (I'm using sarcasm with total love here.)

Or you can make a new choice. Changing where you function from and clearing limiting beliefs can be as simple as affirming, "I choose to change. I refuse to function from that limitation anymore."

Our awareness about the issue, bringing it out of the subconscious (or even anti-consciousness–where you were refusing to look at an issue) and into the light, creates change. Actively choosing to change is the most powerful creation of our future.

However, you can become aware of your limitations and use them as a further limitation. For example, you might have just learned you are afraid of success because you will outshine your BFF. You might worry that if you become a millionaire you will no longer get to kvech on the couch about the biz together over a glass of wine, or she will resent you and the friendship will break, then you wouldn't want to take this as evidence you should keep holding back. You don't get to use it as a conscious excuse now that you're aware of it! Well, you can–you have a choice! But I suggest you choose something that will create your future. I think if you're still with me at this point, you know you want to create something different too.

2. Verbalize your choice to clear it

After you've chosen to move out of that energy, to fire it from your life, verbalize your choice by saying, "Everywhere I believe 'I can't be a millionaire author because my books aren't good enough' [insert your limiting belief], I now clear from all levels, layers, dimensions, and lifetimes."

Speaking and affirming this out loud sets a clear intention both for yourself and the Universe.

3. Visualize it leaving your energetic field

- Close your eyes and imagine your body surrounded by a giant ball of light that extends three feet beyond you in all directions.
- Picture, feel, or sense every place in your body or within the field where the core wound might be hanging out. You might see it as a cloudy film that murks up your energy field, or a place where energy is more dense or dark. You might feel it. Even if you don't see, feel, or experience anything, make it up–your imagination will do the work necessary to clear it from your field. Believe in yourself even if there's no tangible evidence.
- Imagine sucking it out with a vacuum or using a giant magnet to draw it out. You could also visualize moving a violet flame through your field to "burn" it all away. Keep sucking or pulling or burning until all the residue and imprinting of that core wound or belief is gone and the energy field appears clear or clean.
- Take a deep breath and exhale out any remaining blockages.
- Repeat this process until you feel lighter or clearer.

4. Flip the script

Replace the limiting belief with an empowering one. Basically, you take your limiting belief, such as, "Money is the root of all evil" and flip it into what will create more for you, like "I make positive changes with my money."

Using our example of "I can't be a millionaire author

because my books aren't good enough," I might replace it with, "My books are amazing, and I attract millions of readers who love them" or "Any author can become a millionaire when they're willing to receive." (Need I remind you that newbie authors writing *Twilight* fan fiction have made millions?)

What we're doing here is creating possibilities.

Speaking of "Positive," we don't want to have a positive or negative charge on anything—pushing or pulling creates another limitation. This belief we hold that something is black or white, right or wrong, good or bad is a destructive notion. When you're trying to create something, you want to have access to all energies. Every decision you make that one thing is good and another is bad limits what you can pull from when you go to create. The Universe doesn't discriminate between good or bad. The Universe contains all that is. So if we want to create the way the Universe does, we want to have access to all that is, which requires staying in flow and away from polarities. The way I see it energetically, every decision you make, every judgment is like building a closet or room to put yourself into. It's constructing walls. When you have all these walls and barriers surrounding you, caging you in, it's much harder to pull things in and receive.

In the example above, using the statement "I make positive changes with my money" probably doesn't have a positive or negative charge on it (despite the use of the word *positive*). If it's a statement that makes you feel open and free, where energy can flow, it's okay. You just don't want to come to a conclusion, like "I only spend my money in ways to help people." Can you feel how that locks something into place? There's an implied judgment that using money to help people is a positive, and using it in selfish ways is a negative.

In fact, some of us could stand to be far more selfish with our money, attention, and time. Rejecting this notion of being *selfish* will not make the world a better place. Taking care of yourself and allowing yourself to succeed and receive abundance will. When you're generous with yourself you can be generous with others, and it won't drain your reservoir. In fact, your reservoir will become limitless.

To avoid polarity, watch for words like *never* or *only* in statements like these:

- "I will never be poor again." In this case, having a charge against being poor will draw poverty to you. Instead of resisting what you don't want, phrase your request to the Universe in terms of what you want to create. For example, "Money flows to me with total ease." Say that out loud and notice how you feel when you speak the words. Close your eyes, relax into it, and say it a few times. You may feel discomfort, resistance, pulling, something is slightly off, or some kind of drag. Lean into that and see if you can feel into what's under the resistance. You may feel total ease and flow. Notice that.

- "I don't have enough money for that" could become "Every dollar I spend comes back to me tenfold." How do you feel when you say that out loud?

- "Bookbub hates me" could become "Bookbub loves me" or if you can't believe that yet, try "Every submission gets me closer to a Bookbub Featured Deal." Does that feel light, or is there

still tension? What statement can you create
that allows you to connect to the belief that you
will have a book on Bookbub if that's what you
want?

- "I'm doing all the things, and it's not
  happening" could be "My time is coming."
  How does that feel?
- "I can't because..." could be "I don't know how,
  but I believe it could happen for me...." What
  do you feel?

To help me balance out polarity, I like to repeat both the
positive and the negative until there's no charge on
either. For example, one of the things that stops me is my
fear of failure and desire for success, so I repeat, "I am a
success. I am a failure. I am a success. I am a failure."
over and over until I don't feel like I have a charge on
either one anymore.

Here's one everyone should try. Repeat "I love money, I love
money, I love money" until you can say it without cringing.
Until you can own it. Be it. Have it. Lee Savino, my co-
author and partner in abundance coaching, challenged me
to this, and it took me a bit of practice until I cleared out the
pipes. Try "I love rich people" (since you're going to be
one!). Practice saying it until you clear any resistance to
those words!

* * *

Additional Clearing Methods

These are the clearing steps I use. If this method doesn't resonate for you, pick one or several of the other clearing methods below to support clearing your limiting beliefs.

Energy clearing sessions

I like to work energetically with almost everything in my life. You can find an energetic healer who will do the work for you. I also provide these in the form of guided meditations and energetic clearings in the monthly membership calls. If you'd like a free taste, I have a ten minute meditation for meeting your word count goal with ease.

You can listen to it here: https://millionaire-author-coaching.teachable.com/p/a-meditation-for-fast-writing.

To join the Author Abundance monthly membership, click here: https://millionaire-author-coaching.teachable.com/p/author-abundance-membership

Emotional Freedom Technique (EFT) or "tapping"

EFT is wonderful at removing disturbances in the nervous system. Anywhere you have developed a charge on something, experience stress in your body, or want to clear a limiting belief or emotion, EFT can help balance your nervous system. I won't attempt to give any lessons on how to use it here as there is a wealth of knowledge and "how-to's" on the internet, including some wonderful Youtube videos. People frequently post favorites in my Facebook group, so be sure you've joined if you want recommendations. One of the members of the group recently shared a six minute tapping video to earn an extra three thousand dollars a month, and she earned exactly that after a month of doing it!

The Sedona Method®

This is a book by Hale Dwoskin that's available in audio format. It presents a really clear, simple five-step method to let go of things. I have a lot of travel anxiety, and I read this book right before a trip once and used the methods on my drive to the airport. By the time I arrived, I was practically floating in total ease and relaxation!

The Access Consciousness Clearing Statement®

This is one I use all the time. It's a series of words that are shorthand for pages and pages of clearings to get at things from all levels, layers, dimensions, time and space. For example, I might have a limiting belief that I don't have enough time in the day to write. As soon as I notice it or catch myself telling someone this sad story, I'll clear it by saying, "I destroy and uncreate the belief that I don't have enough time in the day to write. Right/wrong, good/bad, POD / POC, all 9, shorts, boys, POVADs and beyonds." I realize none of that means anything, or it sounds like some kind of witchcraft spell, but that's because it's shorthand for clearing the limiting belief everywhere it might be stuck. You can read what it all stands for at https://theclearingstatement.com

Hypnosis or Self-hypnosis

I'm a huge fan of self-hypnosis for reprogramming mindset. I've used it to rid myself of migraines and to birth both my babies naturally at home (my second in just forty minutes from the first contraction–my husband had to catch him because the midwife hadn't arrived yet!). There are so many great resources online for guided hypnosis. You can also get a hypnotherapist to work with you and give you a recording to listen to at night to clear your limiting beliefs and patterns.

Access Bars®

This clearing method requires a practitioner to run the bars on your body. The session uses 32 energetic points on the head to clear limiting beliefs and energy blockages. I'm a huge fan. My first session opened up my intuition in a new powerful way and cleared a huge block I had around making myself small so others wouldn't feel "less-than". I didn't notice the change immediately, but the next time I went to teach my dance class, it was suddenly clear to me how much I cloaked my own brilliance for fear of outshining others.

Access Bars sessions can treat anxiety and depression and clear up to ten thousand limiting thoughtforms in just one session!

I've had some magical experiences with Bars. One time a friend had shared with me an upsetting story about how a colleague had stolen all her clients. Offended on her behalf, I proceeded to retell the story to a few people, spreading the drama of the situation. After getting my Bars run, the next time I opened my mouth to tell that story, I clearly heard a voice in my head say, "don't ever tell that story again."

I instantly understood why–I know enough about energy to know that I was just adding more drama and strife to the situation instead of fostering any kind of meaningful change. Having my Bars run somehow cleared out my points of view enough so that my internal wisdom could come through to guide me.

How do I choose which clearing method is right for me? And Why does this matter?

Use your inner guidance system. Pick the one that feels the most fun, the lightest or brightest to you or the one you're most drawn to. Or try them all!

When we tell a story, we become the energy of the story, and we contribute to the energy of it. When we resist or are in the energy of limiting beliefs, we can't become the energy of the thing we most want. When we can get to the state of harmony with a thing, we can be in the energy of it. For instance, if you have any limiting belief about the statement *"money flows easily to me,"* money cannot flow easily to you. If you believe that *money flows easily to you*, it will. If you believe that becoming a *USA Today* best-selling author is beyond you, it will be. When you can be the energy of a *USA Today* best-selling author, you will be. Let's see just how one author became the energy of the list.

Case Study: Molly O'Hare – Hitting the List

Romance author Molly O'Hare contacted me for a private coaching session before making her second run at the *USA Today* list. She'd made a previous attempt and didn't hit it. As a member of our Author Abundance monthly calls, she understood that her energy was bogged down by the disappointment and sense of failure she carried, and she wanted to clear that energy, so she could get aligned with her goal.

During our session, she admitted one of the reasons hitting the list was so important to her was to "prove" she was good enough, smart enough, worthy. Like me on my first list run, she wanted to hit the list to show she was legit. A real author. To earn those letters.

But to her, it was even more important. Molly had a learning disability as a child, and one particular therapist had damaged her self-worth as a teen by telling her she'd never be able to work a professional job. Part of healing that wound for herself and others was writing the book *Learning Curves,* which featured a heroine like herself–a curvy, learning-divergent teacher who finds love with a single dad.

This was the book she had received a Bookbub promotion for–the one she hoped to hit the list with this time.

I knew the energy of proving actually blocks rather than creates because you're coming from lack. If you need to hit the list to prove you're legit (and believe me, I'm not judging–I felt this so hard!), then your energy is in a place of "not legit yet". You're telling the Universe you're not worthy, rather than being the energy of a valued, *USA Today* (or *New York Times*) bestselling author.

Molly agreed. "The very first run, I reeked desperation. I can see that now. I was so desperate to prove to everyone else that I belonged here versus proving to myself. And I was doing the whole looking for the external validation from them to prove that I belong here."

I knew, really, there was no one we had to convince that Molly was worthy, except Molly. Particularly, that traumatized teen inside her who was told she'd never amount to anything. I suggested she energetically give that teen the book *Learning Curves*. To show her what she'd become–a published romance author capable of writing incredible books. Molly wept as she had a vision of her teenage self curling up in the corner of the therapist's office with the book–so vindicated by this proof of what she would go on to do.

After our call, Molly continued to do the difficult energetic work. The day before the list week began, she took a long "spiritual shower" (isn't that the place where we all can tap into the divine?) As she describes it, "I stood under the shower, and I had a come-to-Jesus moment with myself. I asked, what would happen if I didn't list? Would I be okay? I realized, *You know what? It doesn't matter if I list or not because at this point, I really do feel like I am there.* I *was* the energy of a *USA Today* Bestseller.

"I decided that in parallel Universes, I am as big as Kristen Ashley, Colleen Hoover, or any of the big names out there. So all I need to do is pull that energy into this Universe, this dimension. I thought, *Well, what is this book?* This book is about my growing up with a disability and feeling so alone. I realized I'm okay if I don't list because the goal of this shouldn't be listing. The goal should be to get a book out that could potentially make someone not feel less than, not feel so alone–like I had. I was in the shower for forty-five minutes. It was right before 12:00 Eastern time. So for the start of the sale, and I got in the shower and I thought, *yeah, you know what? I'm okay with whatever happens, however it happens, I'm going to be okay with it now.*"

I often think it's ironic that the moment we no longer need something is when it can come in. You've heard the story over and over again about couples trying to conceive, and the moment they adopt, they also get pregnant? It's because they finally released the resistance to the pregnancy. They step into the energy of *now we are parents* rather than *why isn't this happening,* and the gates open.

That's why Molly's aha moment in the shower–where she realized she already was enough and had nothing to prove either way–was so important. She released the desperation, the need to have this external validation to prove something, and stepped into, *I am already there.*

She continued to do bad-ass energetic work for the entire week to keep herself aligned. Any time she faced feelings of disappointment or despair or believing she wasn't "enough," she used EFT or "tapping" to clear. She meditated, calling in the energy of highly successful romance authors like Colleen Hoover or Kristen Ashley and thanking them for paving the way for her success. Aligning with it.

She used a meditation I taught in the monthly calls to connect with the energy of her book, *Learning Curves*, and ask it what it needs–ad spend, newsletter swaps, etc. "It would always just say *believe, just believe. Trust me.* And little Molly was always over in the corner at that therapist's office where we gave her the book, happily reading it or just cheering me on. I knew no matter what happened, she was proud at that moment."

During one powerful meditation, Molly had a vision of all her books start changing their covers to show *USA Today Bestselling Author* on them.

Molly also used the "Law of Assumption" for daily goals and to get her Facebook ads approved and serving at a low cost.

"Tuesday, right before I went to bed, I said, *I assume I'm going to sell over 2000 U.S. copies of* Learning Curves. Then I went to bed. The next morning I looked, and I had sold 2100 U.S. copies. Because I got that boost of confidence with my law of assumption, I was able to do it every single day."

Molly journaled every day, and at the end of each journal entry, she ended with *I'm already enough. I am already enough regardless of what happens.* So she affirmed it didn't matter if she didn't list, it didn't matter if she did list. She was already enough.

"I got so many emails from people who had learning divergent kids who have gone through the same thing. I got another email from someone recounting that a counselor had done the exact same thing to her. I didn't feel alone anymore. The Universe had given me all these people so that I no longer feel alone.

"Four years ago when I published *Hollywood Dreams*, if you would have told me that I would have gotten a book to sell more than ten copies, I would have laughed at you. I was that learning divergent kid with severe dyslexia, and that just wasn't in the cards for me."

On the day the *USA Today* Bestseller list came out and Molly realized she'd hit, she had that sense I often feel when I manifest something–both excitement that it happened, but also the calm "of course" feeling–because part of you knew you'd receive it all along.

Her joy wasn't just about hitting the list, though. In the process of doing the energetic work to align with that goal, she'd discovered the more important feeling of self-worth and pride for her work.

"My whole entire life, I had to sit at my desk when people got called up to get their honor roll ticket and their stupid bumper sticker that their parents got to put on their car saying *my child is an honor roll student at so and so school*. I never got to have that feeling. But when the list came out, I finally felt what that feeling was like," Molly said. "But it was also the icing on the cake."

"We write love stories that end up in success because the couples end up together. *Learning Curves* is a fight song book. It's about finding new ways with your challenges and proving that you aren't less just because someone said you were. It's always been about finding your inner strength when you might not necessarily have the outer strength. **So it was always meant to be the book that hit the list.**"

Chapter 4

Money Blocks

Money blocks are the limiting beliefs, resistance and bad feelings we have around money, wealth, and abundance. Step one of manifesting abundance in your author career is to "Clear the Deck" of all your negative thoughts and feelings around wealth. If you don't address those wounds, limiting beliefs and blocks, you won't have much of a chance at creating something new. It's like trying to build a new house on quicksand; your beautiful structure will sink.

Most of us have been programmed to hate money. To believe that having money, especially EXTRA money, is a source of evil in the world. Billionaires are vilified.

Even when we think we've done the work, we believe we want money, there are still those beliefs running in the background, haunting our subconscious programming.

The rich are portrayed as greedy, selfish, ungenerous, harmful to the environment—you know the picture. None of us want to be that guy.

It's impossible to live in this reality without thousands of beliefs about money and wealth. There's so much judgment around it! In fact, just talking about it is considered rude or gauche.

Screw that. We're talking about it here.

I guarantee you this: unless you are already massively wealthy and feeling abundant, you harbor many blocks and wounds with money. How often do you base a decision entirely on money? Or reject an opportunity because you believe you can't afford it? What if you believed, instead, that you can have everything you desire, even if you don't know how it will come?

Yes! Even if you don't know how it will come. You don't have to know where it's going to come from. Alignment with the energy of it, of the possibility of it, is what's key.

A pervasive misconception around money is that if you allow more into your life, someone else will go without. Like it's cake at a birthday party, and if you take more than your allotted piece, the last kid served won't get hers. There's the belief that greed is the downfall of humanity, and that may be true.

Greed is a different energy than abundance. Greed carries that energy of desperation and lack. Sticking with the birthday party theme, it's the rushing in after the candy spills from the piñata. In this case, you don't wait your turn to get your allotted piece. Every kid knows that if you don't swoop in and scoop up as much candy as you can as fast as you can, you miss out. Can you sense the lack in that scenario? Even though there's actually plenty of candy for everyone–usually way more than any kid actually needs or wants?

I had a hard time reconciling my desire for abundance with not wanting to be greedy.

I'm an environmentalist. I read *The Lorax*. I've witnessed how greed has led to the devastation of our natural resources. I didn't want to align in any way with the people behind the companies responsible for that kind of raping and pillaging of our sweet Earth.

But me refusing wealth doesn't help that situation. In fact, I can do more with money to aid the environment than I can without it. I started with my own home, installing solar panels, rain harvesting, and greywater systems. Buying an electric car to reduce emissions and our dependence on fossil fuels. I fund reforestation efforts, and I have dreams of using my money to invest in my community's biodiversity.

In her book *We Should All Be Millionaires*, Rachel Rodgers points out the good that we can do with our money. "Making money and making the world a better place are not mutually exclusive," she says.

> "If we as women are truly passionate about improving our lives, making the world a better place for our children, and getting equity for all marginalized people, then we need to step up and make bank."
>
> — Rachel Rodgers

If you want to make significant money as an author, you have to address your money blocks, or you won't allow abundance to flow to you.

Here are just a few of some really common limiting beliefs around money that affect the amount of money you can receive from your books.

I Can't Afford That

How often do you dismiss something without really letting yourself consider it because you believe you can't afford it?

The truth is, we can afford or figure out how to have anything we want, no matter what our circumstances are. I have a good friend who was practically penniless after her divorce. Her house was foreclosed on, she was jobless and received no child support from her ex, but she managed to manifest house sitting jobs in beautiful expensive homes, surrounding her children with luxury while she figured out her next step.

What if instead of making decisions based on money, you made the choice based on what really excited or lit you up? On what contributed most to you? Try asking yourself the question: *if money were no object, what would I choose?* Sometimes it is the cheaper version of something: sometimes it's not. At least you get clarity on what you really want vs. what you think you can afford.

If you can't believe you can have something because of finances or other circumstances, you can also window-shop in the meantime. Try allowing yourself to have the energy of the thing you desire right now. Just say, "I'll have that" and pretend you already do. Receive the energy of it.

After my divorce, but before I was ready to date, I was drawn to a man. I'm sure he would've gone out with me–he definitely gave me the signals–but I was absolutely not in a place to initiate anything. I didn't want to date. I was exhausted from my past marriage and just needed to heal. I chose instead to receive the energy of having sex with him. I closed my eyes and invited in the energy. My body tingled. I received his energy as a contribution. It felt wonderful! You can have the energy of anything you desire right now, simply by receiving it. We'll talk more about this in step five.

Catch yourself when you're saying or thinking "I can't afford that" or other variations like:

- That's too expensive.
- I don't have the money for that.
- It's out of my price range.

Notice if you don't even consider things above a certain price range. When I was looking for a house, I was looking in a range far below what I actually ended up paying because I simply didn't believe I could afford anything more. My real estate agent kept showing me this house, and when I realized it was mine, I figured out a way to make it work. My life completely changed as a result of me re-envisioning my self-image to include a beautiful home outside my price range. It was an upgrade that continues to contribute to my life in so many wonderful ways.

Every time you catch one of these thoughts, try replacing it with one of the following script flips:

I'm choosing to spend my money on other things right now.

This is a good one to say to children if you have them. So you're not affirming that your family can't afford something, you're showing that not buying something is a choice you're making in the moment.

I'm having that.

No need to specify whether you're having it now or later, whether you'll buy it or will magically receive it. You're just affirming that you'd like that thing you may not have the funding for at this particular moment, and you are open to receiving it any way it shows up.

Everything I spend comes back to me tenfold.

If you decide to pay for something that you don't feel like you can afford–perhaps for an unexpected bill or just something you want that is pricey–affirm this when you're spending the money. Or try one of the following:

I'm investing in myself / my future / my business.

I'm worth it.

And when you say it, notice how you feel. If you notice drag, lean in, and work with that until you clear.

I Have to Save Every Penny

This was my mom's limitation, and one I mimicked until I actively chose out of it. It comes from lack–the belief something terrible will happen and you'll need that money in the bank. I'm not against saving. On the contrary, I've been learning to make saving as fun as spending lately, but you want to be mindful of the energy behind the saving. Is it out of fear? Or is saving fun? Putting money in my kids' college funds is fun for me. I get excited thinking of their future, and I'm so happy and honored to be able to help them this way. It's a very different energy than believing I need to keep every cent in case the royalties dry up tomorrow, and I'm stuck with nothing. Honestly, that is a fear I still have to continually clear. But I remind myself that I created this revenue stream, and if it went away, I could create another. I have trust in myself and trust that the Universe has my back.

Be on the lookout for saying or thinking things like:

- You never know when disaster will strike.
- Tomorrow it could all be gone.
- A penny saved is a penny earned.

- I'm socking it all away for retirement.
- I need to stockpile for the what ifs.

Try one of these script flips:
I am the source of my abundance. If I need more, I can create it.
I can't take it with me.
I'm worth it.

You Should Spend It While You Have It

This is the opposite of the previous money wound. It's where you feel the need to pay off your bills, buy the things you're lacking and spend the money as quickly as it comes in because you aren't comfortable HAVING or keeping it.

You've probably heard the statistic that lottery winners are more likely to file bankruptcy within three to five years after winning than the average American. Sometimes people can receive money, but they aren't comfortable hanging onto it, especially if it all comes in fast, like a lump sum. It might come down to feeling like they don't deserve the money that they received if it was won or inherited. Or maybe they didn't spend time changing their self-image to include having money. Being rich. Keeping their bank account full.

After healing from my mother's mindset of saving every penny, I went to the opposite. I didn't overextend myself, or spend money I didn't have, but the moment money came in, I would redistribute it. I would instantly pay off all my bills, then I would spend the rest on my shopping list of things I wanted. It seemed I still wasn't comfortable simply *having* money. I'd figured out the receiving money part, and the spending was coming along just fine, but *keeping* it wasn't a familiar energy. My friend and psychic advisor, Simone Gers, told me it was because saving didn't seem fun. I needed to think of it as "building my treasure chest" instead of that boring, tightwad activity my mom had advocated. So I renamed my savings account "Treasure Chest" in my bank portal, and made putting at least ten percent in there each month a priority. Watching it grow is now as fun as spending money for me.

Consider paying yourself first before you buy the things you need or pay the bills that are waiting. Set up a savings account that is a place to grow money just to keep, just to have, not for anything specific.

Watch out for behaviors or beliefs like:

- There's no guarantee I'll make this much again. (Authors feel this so hard!)
- I need to pay my bills as soon as they come in.
- You have to spend it while you have it, you don't know when it will come in again.
- This windfall could've been a fluke.
- This was my big payday, so I need to grab all the things I put off buying before.
- I'm feeling flush, so I should spread the wealth. (There's nothing wrong with generosity, but did you pay yourself first?)

A script flip on this could be:
Money comes to me and sticks.
I love having money in the bank.
I pay myself first (and put away a percentage before I pay anyone else)

There's Only a Certain Allotment of Abundance

I'm not sure where this idea originates, but it's pervasive. The concept is there's not enough to go around, so if you have more, someone else will have less.`

Sometimes it shows up as a superstitious belief, like there's a cosmic balancing of scales that must take place. You might think if you get greedy or lucky, something bad will happen.

The same day my author friend Tess Summers hit the *USA Today* list—a long-time dream for her—there was a local tragedy in our hometown. Her husband is a law enforcement officer, and one of his colleagues was shot in the line of duty. When she and I went out to celebrate hitting the list, she shared with me that she couldn't help feeling like it was the Universe balancing out the good thing with something bad.

I countered that there are always bad things happening in the world, and they aren't caused by good things happening. We have the tendency to feel guilty about celebrating our wins or having abundance when someone else is suffering. Maybe it feels uncompassionate or unkind.

We touched on this a little before. It's the idea that somehow your having wealth deprives someone else of it. This is where I remind you that when you breathe oxygen, it does not deprive anyone of oxygen. Nor does standing in the sun take away the sun from anyone else. Just like oxygen and sunshine, abundance is energy available to everyone. It's not a limited resource. If everyone felt abundant, our economy would soar, and there would be more jobs and more millionaires.

When Covid first hit and we went into quarantine,

there was a lot of financial contraction in everyone's world. Remember the toilet paper shortage? It was literally a result of people going into fear about not having enough and rushing out to clear the shelves. The truth was, there would've been enough if they hadn't freaked out and stocked up. This is prime evidence of where lack mentality about toilet paper literally made it disappear.

I realized that the state of the economy was really just a collective state of mind. When people contract their abundance mindset, they stop spending money, and the economy slows. When they expand, it flows. Of course, I consider my beliefs to be woo-woo, and I generally keep them to myself, but economists actually say the same thing. According to the Brookings Institute[1], inflation expectations–the rate at which people expect prices to rise in the future–matter because actual inflation depends on what we expect it to be.

What's more, when you choose abundance for yourself, it becomes *more available* to everyone else because that energy is in the field. You are contributing to abundance consciousness for everyone on the planet.

Think about when you're having a hard time, the person you want to be with is someone who reinforces what's possible, not what sucks in the world. You don't need a friend to dig a hole and sit in it with you. You need one who will offer you a hand to climb out of it.

I have to be careful because I'm very empathic. It's easy for me to start to resonate with the emotional content I take in. Listening to the news almost always results in me crying over someone else's pain. I just have to remember that resonating with their pain doesn't take it away, it only adds to more pain on the planet. My gift is staying cheerful, bringing my light, and lifting others with my energy.

Watch out for thoughts or beliefs like

- I can't have it all.
- Great wealth requires great sacrifice (of time, labor, health, etc).
- It's not right for me to be happy when others are suffering.

Script flip:
My joy and abundance adds to others' joy and abundance.

I can have it all.

My joy is a gift to the world.

Money Is the Root of All Evil.

Money is power. It's freedom. It's the medium we use to buy many of the things we want in life. Is it evil? No. Money is just money. Yes, greed for it can cause people to act in evil ways. But you won't. You will do wonderful, amazing things with your money. You will be a huge contribution to the planet simply by allowing yourself to have it, and I know you will use it for good.

When I first hit six figures, I upgraded my clothing. A friend who is a fashion expert took me to the Off Saks and styled me in a dozen new outfits. The trouble was, I was like the lottery winner who couldn't hang onto the money. My self-image hadn't evolved to me having money to dress myself well. I wasn't comfortable in my new clothes. I identified as the hippie / granola mom. The artsy creative who wore graphic tees and Chucks. I was an active PTA mom at a magnet school. I remember standing in my new sparkly silver and black Steve Madden sneakers in the school courtyard feeling like I must look like a "Foothills Mom". The ones who, I imagined, take Pilates during school hours and don't work outside the home because they have rich husbands.

It's not that I think Foothills moms are bad or even that different from me. I mean–hey–I do take Pilates during school hours sometimes! But I had a certain judgment about them. In my mind, they were conservative. They were only worried about themselves and their families, rather than the community as a whole. I mean, they probably chose to live in the Foothills to get away from the lower-income population, I thought. They didn't send their kids to a magnet school to make a difference for the kids who lived in the lower income neighborhoods. I guess, deep down, I still believed rich people sucked. They were greedy, snobby, wanted to get ahead, and didn't care about the rest of the world.

It took a while for me to feel okay with having nicer things and to realize that me having those nicer things didn't automatically turn me into that Foothills Mom archetype I had judged.

You don't have to become corrupt to want to have money. What if you chose to be a benevolent rich person? What if you used your wealth to create change in the world? What if you showed a generosity of spirit that forever changed people's lives?

Check in with yourself to see if you have any beliefs like:

- Money will change me, corrupt me.
- I don't want to become a snob, a rich bitch.
- My morals have to change or degrade to align with having money.
- Rich people are stingy.

- Rich people make money off the backs of others. They destroy the environment. They only care about themselves.

Try one of these script flips:

I will do amazing things for my community with my wealth

Money is a vehicle for good.

I use money to make a difference in my life and the lives of others.

No Matter What I Do, I Can't Get Out of Debt / Get Ahead

Have you heard of the happiness set-point theory? It's the idea that each person has a fixed level of happiness, and they don't go much higher or lower than it on a day-to-day level. Well, **you may also have a set point for debt or income.**

I was raised with the idea that debt was dangerous and should only be taken on very carefully, so my debt set-point was very low. I saved up to buy used cars and always paid off my credit card bill at the end of the month. When I married, my ex-husband had a different comfort level with debt. In his mind, credit was something you used to get the things done that you wanted to do. It was your money working for you. We were both entrepreneurs, and he showed me how we could leverage our credit to purchase start-up equipment or invest in our businesses. For a while, I got comfortable with carrying a balance on our credit cards. No matter what happened, I always seemed to have about a ten thousand dollar balance on them. It was my new set-point.

I mentioned it one day to a friend who had a little judgment of my situation when she declared, "I would never carry debt on a credit card. I just don't believe in that." Going back into shame about my situation, I very quickly figured out how to get that debt completely paid off within a matter of months and haven't carried debt on a credit card since. As you can see, it's all a choice. There were years there when I felt like I couldn't do anything to get rid of that debt, it just always seemed to stay the same until I just changed my mind about it and took care of it.

The same goes for income. You might have a certain range you know you need to live on and beyond that, it seems like you never can make much more. May I point out that you probably also don't ever make much less? Unless there's some significant circumstance, I'll bet you always figure out how to bring that amount needed in.

So...the answer to getting out of debt or getting ahead might be as simple as changing your set point. Your comfort level with the debt or the income.

When my kids were young, we lived for many years on around $35,000-$40,000 a year for a family of four. That's not even considered middle class, yet I never felt poor. We owned a home and cars and took budget vacations and never did without. I was basically comfortable with that income level. Sure, I wanted more, that's why I focused on marketing my books, but as a set point, it worked. Now my set point is much higher. When I don't see six figures on my BookReport for the month, I have to clear any contractions that happen in my world to keep myself from going into lack mentality and wondering what's going wrong or fearing it will all dry up tomorrow.

So how do you change your set point? It's intention with a bit of power and potency behind it. The origin of the word "decision" is literally "to cut off". When you decide to eliminate your debt, or when you decide to change your income set point, you're cutting off all other possibilities.

My co-author and bestie Lee Savino says the first time she made six thousand in one month from her books, she just decided, "I'm a six-figure author now. I'll never make less than eight thousand a month in royalties again." She had no reason to make such a decision based on her past experience, other than the fact that the six thousand dollar month was a February, which she figured was a short month and could have been even higher had it been longer. She hadn't ever made eight thousand in a month. But she chose that day, and it instantly became her new set point. Her new reality. She has never made less than eight thousand a month since.

Let's go back to the lottery winners. Seventy percent of them end up broke within seven years of winning, and one-third go on to declare bankruptcy. I think this could be related to their set point. They were able to attract a huge sum of money, but because their set point and their self-image hadn't adjusted, they weren't comfortable having or keeping it. They went back to their set-point. Their comfortable range of living.

Other Set Points

Set points show up in other areas of an author business as well. You've heard the story about the four-minute mile? For nearly one hundred years, runners had tried to run a mile in less than four minutes and just couldn't seem to do it. It had become a psychological barrier. As soon as Roger Barrister broke that record in 1954, others immediately followed. Once they saw it could be done, once they knew what was possible, a thousand other runners joined the ranks.

Hitting top 100 on Amazon was like that for a group of us. We were all in a Facebook ads course together, learning how to use ads to launch Kindle Unlimited books with a big bang. Hitting top one hundred was a marker for success, but none of us had hit it. That was something reserved for other authors. The special ones. Not us.

I started writing kinky erotic romance and somewhere along the line I got it in my head that only "mainstream" romance authors could top the charts. My work was too kinky. It would always remain relegated to the naughty closet. Do you notice the defeat and limitations packed into those beliefs?

Then someone in our group hit it with her release–the very savvy Stasia Black. As soon as we watched her do it, everyone did it. Lee Savino and I followed almost immediately behind with one of our Bad Boy Alpha books, then others in the group hit it until it became the norm. We all hit top one hundred with our new releases.

Watch out for other set points like:

- My books always hit X rank on Amazon
- I will never get a Bookbub
- I don't have my "letters" (*USA Today, WSJ,* or *NYT* list)

Try these script flips:

Every book I write hits the top 100.

Bookbub loves me–I know exactly when to apply and always get a featured deal.

I am a **USA Today / WSJ / NYT** *best-selling author.*

I'm a 7-figure author.

It's Wrong to Have More Than I Need

This belief is embedded into many religions. Remember the New Testament quote, "it is easier for a camel to go through the eye of a needle than for someone who is rich to enter the kingdom of God"?

It is not wrong to desire more than you have or need. It is, in fact, your natural urge as a human being. We always want more. We are always seeking to improve, to grow, to expand. We want to experience life to its fullest.

I hit my goal of earning seven figures a year as an author, and as soon as I did, I asked to double it. Because I needed more money? No. Because it's fun to create. It's fun to succeed. Would it make sense for me to just stop writing now that I earned a million? To stop doing what I love? To shut it off, shut it down?

Of course not!

But even as I write this, I cringe a little, feeling like I'll be judged for one million a year not being enough. I'm so grateful for what I've received, but it's never enough. I always want to continue growing, stretching, learning, developing. Money is just one of the ways to measure success. It's a reflection of that growth.

For those who are religious, one of the things that helped me resolve these doubts and questions in my early adulthood was Julia Cameron's spiritual principles of creativity in *The Artist's Way*. Basically, she presents the idea that creation is an act of God, so when we create (and every manifestation is a creation), we are returning that gift. She says, "Our creative dreams and yearnings come from a divine source. As we move toward our dreams, we move toward our divinity."

If you haven't read the book, I highly recommend it. If nothing else, the prescribed morning pages and artist's dates will enhance your life and open the flood gates to having more.

- When is it enough?
- Nobody needs to have that much money.
- There's something wrong with you if you have to have more than you need.

Script flip:

There's always enough and always more to have.

Creating abundance is divine.

Making money is my favorite thing. (I don't know if that's really the flip of anything, but it came to me as a fabulous affirmation).

I Don't Deserve This Much Success / Wealth

This question of deserving gets delivered to us quite early in life. Babies don't come into this world wondering whether they deserve love or food or care. But children pick up very quickly how much or how little their caregivers and world will deliver.

My mom was born on a farm during the depression and was a compulsive saver. How you behaved with money was wrapped up in morality with her. She was raised in that puritanical belief that hard work and modesty would create enough prosperity to take care of yourself and others. Good people didn't have debt or need or want from others. They didn't borrow money. My grandmother didn't own a credit card until she was in her eighties, and it was only to buy a plane ticket! They were never showy or extravagant. They made ends meet.

My mom never allowed herself any luxuries. When she moved in with me for hospice care at the end of her life, her social worker suggested she pay for our cable bill, so she could watch her favorite show. We didn't have cable TV, and she felt like a burden, so the social worker reasoned that it would allow her to feel like she was contributing and also give her the gift of watching *The Good Wife* (this was before the days of Netflix in every home, of course). She hemmed and hawed over the thirty dollars a month it would cost.

When I took her to an attorney to prepare her will, I was shocked to find she had three-quarters of a million in the bank, leaving my brother and me with a decent inheritance. She'd never made more than thirty thousand dollars a year at her job, so she'd accumulated all that through saving and careful investment—the lessons she taught me about money.

Those weren't bad lessons. They caused me to invest in real estate by age twenty-five and max out my 401k contributions at work. But they never made me feel abundant. They taught me to function from lack. After the visit to the attorney, I brought up her deliberation over the cable bill and how it seemed silly when she had so much money sitting there, and she told me she was afraid she'd end up in assisted living, which could wipe out that savings quickly. Her fear was justified, of course, but functioning from fear never creates more. It attracts more lack. My mother died without enjoying her money, other than to watch her favorite show in the three months before she died, and to know she provided for her grandchildren.

What about me? Did my sudden inheritance make me feel wealthy?

It should have.

But then... my aunt flew out to help me with the funeral and gave me the dire warning not to spend any of that inheritance... (because, you know, same money wounds). So I didn't. I spent a tiny bit. I signed my daughter up for piano lessons (an extravagance I hadn't been able to afford) because I knew my mom wanted her granddaughter to play.

My husband at the time felt a bit more abundant than I did. He talked me into using the money to buy a rental property in Taos, where he worked the summers. I could justify the purchase as a decent investment and rationalize it to my aunt and uncle, so we went forward with it. But when I mentioned to anyone that we were able to buy this house, I would always preface it with "my mom died, so..." to prevent anyone from thinking I was lucky. Or abundant. Like the house was my consolation prize for losing my mom, not a choice I'd made to live in an abundance mentality instead of lack. Because honestly? I still didn't believe I deserved a summer vacation house in Taos. Only rich bitches had that, and I wasn't willing to be that yet.

A few years later–and after quite a bit of money wound clearing–I separated from my husband and started looking for a new home. I could conservative with money the way my mother taught me. I could sell off the Taos house, downsize my current residence, buckle down and be cautious. After all, I was an author. My income was never guaranteed. Shouldn't I prepare for disaster, as my mother had?

I certainly heard my mother's voice in my head with that advice.

But I'd done enough work on my blocks to know that wasn't going to create the future I was dreaming of.

I didn't want to downgrade my housing. After working on my money blocks, I was tired of believing I didn't deserve more. I figured if I was making a move, it should be up, not a lateral move, or worse, to something smaller. I asked the Universe for help, and it delivered. I had to think creatively and figure things out, but I opened up to the Universe, tapped into my inner guidance, and got the message that I should sell some of my mom's farmland in Iowa and use the rest of my inheritance—yes, the one my aunt told me not to spend—to buy myself a big, beautiful house. More house than I needed. A bigger house than my current residence.

A castle.

It was a leap for me. I tried to tell myself my mom would want me to use her money to take care of myself and raise her grandkids, but honestly? She wouldn't approve of the extravagance. And that's okay. Because I approve. I decided I was worth it. Making that choice has made *all the difference* in my money reality. It sent a powerful signal to the Universe that I am worth it. That I deserve nice things. That I'm allowed to treat myself.

Every time you honor yourself, the Universe responds in kind and honors you. It brings more abundance, more things you like. Fewer things you don't want.

When I bought my castle, money didn't shut off. God didn't strike me dead for spending it. My abundance didn't put someone else out on the street. In fact, by choosing for myself, I put that possibility into the energetic field for everyone else. For you, reading this book. Every time we choose abundance, we make it more available for others to do the same. Taking care of yourself is a gift to all of humanity.

More and more, I believe I'm allowed to have money. It will stick. I deserve it. I welcome it. *I'm willing to receive it.*

Other examples might be:

- That happens to other people, not me.
- I'm not special enough, good enough to have all that.
- Struggle is part of being an artist.
- I shouldn't_____.

Script flip:
> ***I deserve it all.***
> ***I am worthy. I am enough.***

I Have to Work Hard for My Money

I confess, I can be a workaholic. Nose to the grindstone, I churn out book after book. The time I'm not writing, I spend marketing my books. There's no rest for the wicked at my house, and I'm sure that somewhere along the line, I bought the idea that this is what it takes to succeed.

> The truth is, you don't have to kill yourself working to be abundant.

You don't have to do anything. **What if you could receive money just for *being*?**

I know logically that sounds preposterous, but just

indulge me for a moment here. If you firmly believe that your hours equal dollars, then you will always be tangled in this mess of hard work to be abundant.

Abundance is an energy flow. It's not a boss checking your timesheet. Your body and being can act as receivers or conduits for money to simply flow to you. That doesn't mean you will sit on the couch and eat bonbons all day long. Or maybe it does! You will follow your gut, know when to act and when to give your creations space to breathe. You'll learn there's a divine timing to things, and sometimes a little space and patience is what it takes, not more hard work or frustration or grind. We will talk more about this concept in Step 6, Let it Be.

In the Author Abundance monthly membership, we had a video call recently about getting our books to go viral on Tiktok. Many were resistant to fully engaging with Tiktok because it felt like another task they would have to add to their already too-long to-do lists. You've heard the advice–we should all be posting three to five videos per week. Or per day, depending on who you talk to.

I led a meditation for going viral on Tiktok and partici-pants were guided to follow their own intuition, to be open to divine guidance of what kinds of videos to post and when, and to not feel like they had to manufacture filler videos beyond that.

What if your entire author business ran that way? You followed your inner guidance and acted when you got the nudge. I find that when I act on nudges like that, the work gets done quickly and easily and doesn't feel like work at all. When I grind at something, when I'm doing a task because I'm "supposed to" or I "have to" or worse–when I put it off because it feels like a slog and then I judge myself for not doing it–that is not creating abundance.

That creates barriers to abundance.

Common refrains we hear that are all worth clearing include:

- Hard work pays off.
- You have to put in the time.
- Hard work is the key to success.
- Time is money.

Script flip:

> ***Abundance flows to me just for being me.***
> ***I live an abundant life.***
> ***I love abundance.***

I'm A Struggling Artist, Not A Sell-out

I identify pretty hard with the struggling artist thing. In college, I studied writing, but I didn't focus on fiction or screen-writing. No, I picked poetry. Because, you know, there's just a rabid audience out there for emo poems about broken relationships. After college, I focused on a career in dance. Modern dance. You know–the form that no one thinks they understand? Yeah. That one.

My joke was that I'd picked the two least-loved and least-understood artforms possible. I would not be filling stadiums for my performances. It seemed I was destined to never make enough to live on from my art. Which was, you know, very Bohemian and cool for me. Good thing I love thrift shops and can pinch a penny until it bleeds.

This idea of the starving artist or the struggling artist who stays true to his or her work and never sells out on their artistic vision just to make a buck is just another story you can choose to buy into or leave behind.

The Arizona Commission on the Arts once organized a professional development day for the Artistic Directors of dance companies in the state. During it, someone posed the age-old question, "Should we be making art or entertaining?" I was struck by the answer of the director of the largest and most successful company in the state: "Good art should be entertaining."

In the writing field, we hear this as "writing to market" vs. "writing from the heart". The truth is, we can do both. We can write what we love, what we want to write, but still gear it toward what's selling. Package it and position it and frame it so it sells well.

My point is, artists don't have to struggle, nor do they have to give up on their vision or art in order to make money. You can make money writing what you love. I guarantee, if you love it, someone else will too. Just don't paint yourself into a box of one or the other. Don't close off your options and abundance flows. Stay open to possibilities and be willing to receive money for your art.

Watch out for these limiting beliefs:

- Nobody wants to read what I want to write.
- I have to sell-out and write ___ because that's what's selling now.
- I have to choose between art and entertainment.
- I have to write to market vs. writing what I love.

Try these script-flips:
> *I write what I love and love what I write.*
> *Abundance flows to me.*
> *There are readers for what I want to write.*
> *I follow my gut to market my books.*
> *If I love it, someone else will too.*

I Could Lose It All Tomorrow

I think a lot of us have this fear of scarcity ingrained in our psyches. We pick it up from our lineages and people and messages all around us. If you're a romance author, you probably often use this wound in love. The hero or heroine refuses to fall in love again because they've been hurt once before. They're willing to deny themselves all the pleasure, the greatness, the glory of having a wonderful relationship because it would hurt too much to lose it again.

As illogical as it is, we see this play out daily. After my divorce, it took me several years to feel like I was ready to give my heart again.

I remember when my first child was born, feeling like I loved her so much it hurt. The hurt part was fearing I'd lose her. Fearing something I loved so deeply could be taken from me. I was shown during a meditation (read—a sleep-deprived download from Spirit) how to expand out, so that love didn't hurt anymore and became more of the infinite / unconditional love of oneness.

Maybe having money seems like it could be equally painful. What if you fall in love with having it, only to lose everything?

After a lifetime of scraping by, of feeling the pain of lack, perhaps it feels too frightening to get "comfortable" having money. You might get used to it, and then it would hurt all the more if it goes away.

I still have to clear this fear away often. I have thoughts like:

- I shouldn't get too used to this level of success.
- I don't want to come to rely on this abundance.
- Amazon could shut down my account, and I'd lose everything.
- It could all evaporate.
- The stock markets could crash.
- I could be in a car accident or get critically ill and be unable to write.
- Fortunes are lost every day.

Sure, all of these terrible *what-ifs* could happen. You know what's also true? If you created it once, you can create it again. You are the master of your destiny and the architect of your life. You determine how much wealth you're willing to have, and you can call it to you now and in the future. There isn't one way to create it, either. It doesn't have to be the sales of that one book or series. If you open up to receive abundance from all avenues, you'll get that magical "multiple income stream" that the financial advisors talk about, which makes you a little more bullet-proof. Or recession-proof. Or losing-it-all-tomorrow proof.

Try one of these script flips:

If I created it once, I can create it again.

It's easy to make more money.
Money always comes back to me.
I am the creator of my fortune and as long as
I'm alive, I'll keep creating.
I am the vibration of abundance.
I resonate with abundance.

Having Money Makes Me A Target

When I first heard Porsche was coming out with an electric car, I was gushing about it to my dad, a car enthusiast. I mean, what could be better–a sexy Porsche combined with green technology that could save the planet. Right?

But my dad shook his head. "There's an advantage to my Lexus," he said. "When I'm in the parking lot, there are plenty of other white Lexus SUVs in the lot. I never stand out."

Um...huh?

But how many of us had this ingrained in us probably from our middle school years?

- Don't stand out.
- Don't attract unwanted attention.
- Don't make yourself a target.

I have two teenagers who work extremely hard to make sure they never stand out or do anything out of the norm.

But think of all the abundance, joy, self-expression, and creativity you might miss out on if you refuse to ever stand out.

Living in fear of having too much attention–or of being seen–can become a huge block to success. Think about it.

You're telling the Universe *"I don't want anyone to see me."* Lean into the idea of being seen. If you're really honest with yourself, are you willing to be seen? Where in your life are you willing to stand out? Do you wear the clothes or shoes or even hairstyle that you want? Do you say what you want? Are you willing to put yourself out there in your life? Part of this fear is a fear of failing in public. Of being embarrassed. Of being mocked. Of shame. Of being picked on. Of feeling bad or shamed for wanting something more.

Will you market your books properly if you're afraid of being seen?

Will you hesitate to put up a Tiktok video or get personal in a newsletter? How can your books go viral if you're hiding, afraid to stand out? How can you attract wealth if you're afraid it will make you a target? Even if you do attract it, will you let yourself have a flashy car if that's what excites you? Or will you buy the one that lets you blend in with the crowd?

What's interesting is that readers, fans, viewers, people in general love experiencing the ups and downs of life.

I got my start writing kinky, erotic fiction. Many of us who write things that aren't considered completely acceptable, or even that aren't literary fiction, take on a "shrouded" energy. People can't find you as easily if you're in hiding!

Maybe you don't want your fiction professor to know you're writing genre fiction, maybe you don't want your religious mother to know you have explicit sex in your books. Whatever reason you may think you have to be embarrassed or hide what you write, consider letting it go and affirming that you're willing to be seen.

I just heard about Paris Hilton's iridescent pink BMW

i8, and I had to look it up to see it for myself (go look it up and see what I'm talking about!). It is a creation of over-the-top charisma. It is unabashedly feminine. Better than a Barbie car (and no, I never had one, but my friend Claudia did, and I was very jealous). Here's a woman who is not afraid to drive the car that feels fun to her or to show the world that she has money.

My energy coach, Erin Chanel, once asked me, "***Are you willing to be seen***?"

I hesitated. Was I? I'd hidden what I wrote for the first few years I was an author, using a pen name. I was afraid the PTA would find out and kick me off the team for the kinky stories that came out of my head. Also, if you're seen, you might be judged. I might get a heap of bad reviews. I might become the laughing stock of romancelandia.

But no, I decided I was ready. I was ready to be seen.

"Yes," I affirmed to her.

As you'll find out when you follow the seven steps to manifesting abundance, the Universe responds swiftly when we get out of our own way. Literally the next day in my local grocery store, I was stopped by a shopper. "Excuse me," she said.

I stopped and turned with a pleasant smile. I expected her to say one of the usual comments I get from strangers. Either "I like your hair" (I had fuchsia streaks at the time) or "I like your purse" (it was a cute colorful Kate Spade back-pack purse). Instead, she said, "I just want you to know that I love your books."

What?!

I couldn't believe it.

"You read my books?"

"Yes, and I love them."

I felt famous. Appreciated. Not so very alone (let's face

it–authoring can be a lonely business!). My willingness to receive had opened up (we'll talk more about that in Step 7 - Honor Yourself). As soon as I told the Universe I was willing to be seen, suddenly there it was, right in my local grocery store–someone who loved my books.

So... are *you* willing to be seen? Are you willing to be seen as a famous author? As a ***millionaire author***?

Or are you afraid the attention you get will be negative? People egging your car at the grocery store, breaking into your house to steal your treasures, or hounding you for auto-graphs? Can you trust that you can also manifest that the attention you receive will be positive, and anything that's less than positive just won't show up in your world because you give it no energy? That doesn't mean there won't be negativity, but you can choose to receive it without it ruffling your feathers. We can use all energy to our benefit, to create something greater. (And more on how to do that in the next chapter.)

You might be blocking book reviews right now because you're afraid of getting bad ones. That keeps the energy of your book hidden to the world, so readers can't find it. Is that what you want? Or can you agree that even the very best, most loved, most successful authors get bad reviews? Your work won't be for everyone, but you can call to it the people who will love your books, which is a win-win for you and them.

If this is an on-going issue for you, I have a ten-minute meditation to help clear this issue that many people have found useful. You can access it through the Author Abun-dance Monthly Membership.

Script Flip:

I am willing to be seen.

I am seen and loved. (Or even, *See me, love me!*)

My face is my fortune. (This helps me with putting myself on Tiktok!)

It is safe to be wealthy. (Or... I am safe and wealthy.)

It is safe to be successful. (Or... I am safe and successful.)

Case Study - Felicity Brandon: Being Seen

USA Today Bestselling Romance Author Felicity Brandon has been a member of our Author Abundance calls from their inception. At first, for her, just getting on a Zoom call and showing her face to her peers was a stretch.

Felicity is a pen name, and she used it as a layer of protection. "My fear of being known was visceral. It's linked into the genre we write [dark romance]." Felicity didn't want people in her life to know she wrote about sex–particularly not kinky sex. She thought, *What will happen if people find out I'm making money from this?* "I could feel myself holding myself back, but didn't know how to untangle those vines I'd got myself wrapped up in."

Through abundance mindset work, she realized, "The more I feared being seen, the more I didn't make money because no one saw my books–no one knew I was writing them."

"I can almost put my finger in the sand and say the exact moment when I started this journey to be seen. It was 2021–we did the first [Author Abundance] call. It was the first time I was open to being seen–before that, no one knew my face or who I was beyond an avatar."

After that, Felicity made the conscious choice to open up to be seen and everything changed from there. "I started to open up to all the possibilities. I made myself a promise to get out there and be open to everything. Let the readers see me, let the readers come." Felicity chose to book a professional photo shoot and posted the photos on social media to show her face to her readers. "I had to let go and release the energy that isn't serving me and be open to the energy of those who DO love my books. It's been wonderful."

Felicity also experienced an income boost, particularly after doing the "Going Viral on Tiktok" meditation that is included in the Author Abundance Library (part of the monthly membership). "I'd literally started on TikTok a week before, I didn't have a clue. When I listened to the meditation, I concentrated on opening up to suggestions and the Universe."

She found a few specific parts of the meditation to be particularly fruitful–releasing the energy we carry in our fields from other people and magnetizing all the energy from potential readers out there on TikTok.

"Later that day, literally a couple of hours later, my sales more than tripled. I can't say I was viral, but–*wow*–something happened." She relates it to opening up and inviting the energy of all these readers and wanting to be seen, which was totally new to her. "The meditation really nailed it. I've done it twice since, and I've doubled my sales both times I've done it. Magic! Thank you, Universe!"

If Felicity could distill all the abundance mindset magic into one thing, it would be gratitude. "The game-changer is just gratitude. Rather than constantly thinking *I don't have four million pounds in the bank yet* or dwelling in comparisonitis, I really look at what I have– a beautiful home, family, a job I love, a hot shower–drilling it back to basics. You realize you're already the most abundant person in the world. The moment I woke up to that, abundance just flew at me faster than I could catch. The Universe said, *she's finally realized–have some more, have some more.*"

Her advice to other authors: "Be really clear on what you do have. Spend your time thinking about what you have and enjoy rather than what you don't have and are scared of. You definitely receive the energy of what you are–what you radiate is what you get back."

"I can literally track back to the time you started doing these calls–it was transformational. **This mindset is forever. I can employ this in every aspect of my life and be happier, with more ease and joy. It's what we all want!"**

Freewriting: Tap into Your Genius

Let's dig into some of your limiting beliefs around money and wealth. What are your money wounds? Get out your journal and a pen. Remember to keep your pen moving across the page without editing or stopping the flow to think.

Write until you have no more to say about the following:

- What beliefs do you have about rich people?
- What will happen if you get rich?
- What do you hate about money?
- What do you love about money?
- I can't be rich because...
- What belief about money or wealth limits you the most?
- What will happen if I am seen as the writer I am....

Now that you've mined your subconscious for limiting beliefs and thought patterns, disrupt them using one or more of the clearing methods described in Chapter Three, "How to Clear the Crud".

Chapter 5

Clearing Resistance to a New Self-Image

W hen I had my second child, we decided it would be better to move out of our 1200 square foot house and into something larger. Because real estate is supposedly a great investment (as it turned out, that was the particular decade where the real estate market remained totally flat!), we wanted to keep our first house and rent it out to pay the mortgage.

The very week I was getting qualified to refinance that mortgage to pull money out for our down payment on the new house, I was laid off from my job as a technical writer. It was definitely one of those instances where the Universe was delivering what I was too afraid to do myself. I was just finishing a four-year certification program to become a Feldenkrais Practitioner, doing movement re-education bodywork, but leaving the security and benefits of my old job was too scary for me. I'd asked the Universe to fix it, and so it had. I was given three months severance, along with COBRA insurance, which Obamacare had just made affordable, and the chance to collect unemployment while I finished my studies and got my new practice started.

But there was no way the mortgage company was going to accept this loan without me having a job. My husband at the time was self-employed, and they'd already told us they wouldn't take any of his income to qualify. I told the Human Resource department the situation. The mortgage company called her that day, and she didn't have to lie—she verified that (on that day) I worked there and what my salary was. She didn't volunteer the information that my employment would be terminated in a week, and they didn't ask. Once again, the Universe delivered.

But then my money wound kicked in when it came to renting out the old house. How many stories have you heard, movies have you seen, or books read where the landlord is the asshole? I didn't even know I had a hangup about landlords, but it seemed I was terribly embarrassed of stepping into this role. I resisted the idea of being a "slum lord" so much that when my tenants didn't pay their rent on time, I would wait days and days before calling and asking very, very nicely if they could please pay their rent because I couldn't pay the mortgage on the house without it. I let them be late without penalty. I never threatened them, it was more like I begged.

Energetically, I was so unwilling to be the person with the financial power, that I pushed the advantages of that situation away and made things difficult for myself at the expense of my family and my own stress-level. As Rachel Rodgers, author of the inspiring book *We Should All Be Millionaires,* would say, those were some "broke-ass thoughts" rather than "millionaire thoughts."

This isn't to go into whether it's right or wrong to be a landlord, to ask for money that's due to you, or to enter the real estate market.

The problem with this situation was that there was an energy I was resisting, and it created a wobble in my Universe.

Any time you resist being something, any time you swear (in any lifetime) "I'll never be that" or "I'll never do that," it causes a restriction in your current world. If you hate manipulative people and have sworn to never be that person, then you're attracting those people into your life because you have a positive or negative charge on it. Any polarity creates difficulty by magnetizing the very pattern to you.

If you never want to be the person who takes the check after the meal and adds it up with a calculator, only paying for their exact portion, you probably find yourself in situations with people like that often. If you never want to be the free-loader who never offers first to pay for the check, you probably have people taking a free ride off you. You're attracting it by having a charge on that behavior or type of person.

When I first tried to get help cleaning my house, I had a hard time hiring someone. It sparked all kinds of shame. Some of the cringe was around the idea that I thought I should be able to clean my own house, but actually a lot of it was created by me not wanting to be rich-bitch who had cleaning people she bossed around. Again, that woman is always portrayed negatively in movies and books.

To help me clear it, I said out loud five times, "I am a rich bitch, I am a rich bitch, I am a rich bitch, I am a rich bitch, I am a rich bitch" and then cleared everything that brought up.

Practice again saying "I love money" out loud five times without getting a weird catch in your throat or reaction in your body. Then have the courage to lean in and do the work to clear what's there.

What judgments are you making about your own life right now? What structures or patterns in your life keep you in the box, doing the same thing over and over again? What beliefs, prejudices, points of view are keeping you small?

Case Study: Alta Hensley - Coming out of the Box

USA Today Bestselling Author Alta Hensley was one of my first friends in the author community. In 2018, she unwittingly picked me up at the airport in Reno for the RT Booklovers Conference only to have me burst into tears telling her I'd separated from my husband the day before. We shared a hotel room for the conference, and, since I was obviously in need of it, did some energy work together in the room.

One of the things we both talked about was our desire to move past our perceived limitations of being seen as merely erotic authors. "As authors, we're such creative beasts, but we're also doubtful," she said when I spoke to her recently. "I was feeling very small and like I couldn't quite break out. I was ready to step out and be more than just a smut author. I wanted to be mainstream."

As I ran her Bars[1], she released the self-imposed limitation she had of being marginalized as an erotic author. "It's been hard for me to feel like I can get out of the small box where I started. But as we meditated, I realized *I* was the one putting myself in that box. I had imposter syndrome—I felt small. I didn't know how to become big. I didn't know what that was. You broke me past my mold."

As we meditated and visualized together, we both saw the word *Empire* for Alta.

"It brought tears to my eyes–it had a soft but powerful feeling. I realized I was holding myself back from having the empire. It was a mental shift that I had to do," she said.

"The minute the conference was over, my career skyrocketed. I'd let go of that blockage. I stepped out of the box and went more mainstream, and my books did better, I expanded as an author. People reached out to me, and I stepped into the contemporary romance world, from the small erotica niche. Visualizing that I could be bigger and I could grow worked!"

Even now, Alta keeps the word *Empire* written on a note at her desk as an anchor or reminder of the energy she wants to embody. "To me it means *think big, be big, don't put yourself in the small box.* Authors think they're small, and they're hoping some day they'll be big instead of being themselves and being big now."

Of course, as for all of us, it's a constant process. "Even now, it's a work in progress," she said. "I still have to keep focusing on the feeling of *Empire*. Being bigger. I have to resist the pull to stay in the small box. I have to keep reminding myself to stop playing small.

"Sometimes I can be my worst enemy–I limit myself. I think thoughts like *oh, I'm only dark romance, and because of my content, I'll never be mainstream.*" She recounted when Skye Warren invited her to write in her world, Alta asked her what heat level she wanted and how she wanted her to write it. "I was coming from a place of thinking I needed to change myself to fit into her world." Of course, Skye told Alta to write it exactly the way she already writes.

"She asked me because of what I was already writing. I started closing myself in thinking I needed to be something different when I was already there!"

Setting an intention, using meditation and visualization, and focusing on a word of the year are tools Alta uses on a regular basis. "I pick a word that starts my year. *Empire* has been my overarching word for a long time, but I've also used Money, Courage, and Focus."

She also sets her intention for a series.

"I get covers made ahead of time, so then the energy is like it's already done."

— *Alta Hensley*

She said, "A lot of what I did with you was stop boxing myself in. I had to stop limiting myself. I go back to the energy of *Empire*–big. I don't need to be small."

Freewriting: Tap into Your Intuition

Freewrite on the following question: **How am I making myself small?**

Make a list or fill a page answering this question: **What are you unwilling to be?**

I'm sure you have very good reasons for not wanting to be all of those things. Or maybe the reasons are not conscious—something you picked up from watching *101 Dalmations* or something your mother, father, grandparents, or teachers believed.

Are you willing to clear all of it, so there is no polarity or charge on any of this, and you can create the abundant life you're asking for? Write a giant yes on the line below or affirm it out loud.

After you mine these prompts, what clearing strategy tools will help you clear these from your field? Lean in and do the clearings.

Step 2: Feed the Fire

Chapter 6

Finding Your Why and Clarifying Your Intentions

T he next step to manifesting abundance is feeding the fire. This is where you get clear on your intentions, find your why and pull in the feelings and energy that manifesting those intentions will bring.

Personally, I hate when books or movies have the hero or heroine walk away from the riches at the end to show their moral character in a positive light. As if that hero or heroine couldn't have taken the money and done amazing things with it?

Of course, you're not going to turn into Ebenezer Scrooge. Think instead of the good you can do with your abundance. The donation to the PTA, reseeding the Amazon rainforest, helping your niece buy her first car. Think about treating your body to nice sheets or clothes. Taking vacations. Never having to worry about unexpected bills. Whatever lights you up, whatever makes you happy, will be a gift to all of humanity and the Earth.

Chances are you already know what you want. That's why you picked up this book. So let's just feed the fire. Imagine your brightest future in total detail, so you can hold the energy and vibration of it and start to have it right now. (More about that in Step 6.)

This is the fun part! You get to brainstorm your perfect life. Keep in mind this can be an ever-evolving map. You're not locking yourself into anything. You can change your targets midstream. You can choose, then refine that choice, or choose something new over and over again. There are no wrong choices, other than having the belief that there are wrong choices.

Let's find your why

Many people aren't motivated simply by being rich. A number in the bank. They are motivated to get their kids through college, quit the day job, buy that new car, and take a dream vacation. Dig even deeper, and you'll find it's actually an energetic feeling they're going for.

It might be having luxury. An end to feeling powerless or worthless. Having freedom. One of the many things money solved for me was the anxiety that I couldn't handle the bumps life threw my way. Like the heater going out in my house. Or my car breaking down. An unexpected hospital visit. Problems are a little easier to face when you have the resources to get yourself out of them with total ease. But the truth is, you don't need money for that. The Universe already has your back, if you choose to believe it, ask for help, and receive the gifts when they come. And you can have the energies right now of luxury, power and self-worth. We'll discuss this more in step 5.

For now, let's have fun dreaming things into existence.

Freewriting: Tap into Your Intuition

Write until nothing more comes out with the following prompts:

- If you had a magic wand and could wave it to transform your life or career in any way, what would you wish for?
- What does your perfect, magic-wanded life look like?
- Where do you want to be as an author in three years?
- Put yourself there—imagine it's already happened. What does your life look like?
- What are you doing differently? Better?
- Is that something you can already integrate today?
- What is one thing you could do immediately that would improve your career?
- What is one thing you could do today that would improve your quality of life and feel abundant?

- What successes and accomplishments you've already had can you honor and celebrate right now?
- How will you reward yourself for meeting your targets?
- What are examples of three perfect Millionaire Author days? (Hint–this makes a great morning exercise, to imagine more and more variations on the perfect day.)

For example, you wake up, and your sexy partner has already made you a perfect, foamy cappuccino. Your assistant texts to tell you all the things she's going to do for you today, and that you don't need to worry about a thing from the administrative end–just focus on your wonderful book. You have a long, uninterrupted shower in which all kinds of creative thoughts download and get you excited for the scenes you have to write. You grab your pre-packed beach bag and walk down to the beach (because you live just a few feet away, of course!) where you sit under an umbrella and write, easily and effortlessly getting way more than your planned word count in for the day. Then you head back home where a massage therapist has already set up to give you a wonderful massage. That night, you stop in at your local bookstore, where you have a scheduled signing, and there's a line wrapped around the building, just for you. You soak it all in, smiling and waving, loving your fans who love you in return...

Okay, that has never been mine, but now that I wrote it for you, I might incorporate that into my dream machine!

Home Play

This week, make your request / demand of the Universe. Ask for help, guidance, awareness, etc. One of my favorite questions is "What infinite possibilities are available in this situation?"

Phrasing Your Request / Intention

The way you phrase your requests of the Universe is important. If you've ever learned self-hypnosis (or parented a preschooler!), you probably learned that you always phrase things in the positive. You don't say "No more headaches" because all the subconscious hears is "headache", and you'll get more of them.

Instead, you should phrase it in the affirmative. *My head feels great, my mind is clear, and my body is in total ease*–or something like that. In the case of a preschooler, telling them what they *can* do (with their voices, with the sand, with their food), versus what they *can't* do always works better. When I taught tap dance to three-year-olds, instead of telling them to stop the holy racket of stomping their feet and creating the worst cacophony on the planet, I would say in a soft, quiet voice "quiet feet," and it worked like magic. The room would fall silent, and I'd have their inquisitive gazes on me, showing they were ready for the next instruction.

When my teenagers issue complaints, I always ask them to rephrase it as a request. Instead of "I'm hungry," I ask to hear something like, "Mom, can we stop for a snack?" I figure by training them this way, I'm setting them up to manifest like mofos with their life requests from the Universe.

Just think about it—how often do we respond to life's problems like my hungry teenagers? Amazon sends us a rights request letter for a book we uploaded (happened to me today—grr), and we want to throw our hands in the air and say, "this sucks."

Yes, it totally does suck. But what's the request? (I'm really having a conversation with myself now because I'd love to transform this particular issue.) The request to the Universe could be "All of my books get uploaded with total ease." When we create a request or intention, we get clear. Sometimes, I'll catch myself (argh... not another rights letter), and it may take me several iterations before I land on what I really intend. That's okay. Revise until your request is clear and feels light.

It's flipping the script again. It's important to remember that you're programming both your own brain, body, and energetic state as well as making a request to the Universe or setting in motion the law of attraction. Every time you complain about something or someone, you invite more of that into your life. You intensify your experience of it. What would you like to request instead?

Get clear within yourself to flip to the channel of what

you *do* want to experience. Phrase your request in the positive.

- *I am a* New York Times *Bestselling Author.*
- *I make seven figures a year from my writing.*
- *I have a PR and administrative team that gives me all the support I could dream of.*
- *My books and stories have been made into movies.*

Notice how the requests are phrased as if they've already occurred rather than as a wish or want?

Think about the word *want*. In its noun form, it means to lack. For example, "That house is in want of repair."

So we don't want to affirm we lack anything!

Once you know what to request and intend and can clearly state it, you may want to lean into it. When you state your request, is there any drag in your body? Your requests may help you identify pesky limiting beliefs that are ripe for removal. Lean in. Clear them out!

Futurecasting

Here's an even juicier way to play. It's a game of **Future-casting.** You pretend the thing you're asking for has already happened.

When my fellow local authors Tess Summers, Misty Malloy, and I made our dream boards together, we played a game called "Futurecasting". We talked about the year like it had already happened, and we'd already achieved all our goals. For example: "Hey guys, remember in 2020 how I 10xed my income and was able to buy that new Porsche?"

We played this game with parking spots when we went

to a book signing in San Diego. We'd pull into a crowded area and start saying, "remember when it was totally packed, but we found a spot with total ease?" and *literally every time*, the spot would just appear. It happened without fail–to the point where Tess said, "This is getting scary."

When I catch myself going down a rabbit hole of anxiety over something I don't want, I'll turn it into a future casting session to reset myself. Last year we adopted two kittens with a case of the sniffles. Because of covid work shortages (or some other mysterious post-pandemic reason), I couldn't get an appointment at any veterinarian to get them seen. I started going down the "this sucks" rabbit hole, thinking we had to go sit at a vet urgent care or hospital all day on the weekend to get them looked at. When I was searching online for an emergency vet center, I noticed there was a drop-in vet clinic at Walmart. Normally hitting Walmart on a weekend is on my list of the last things I want to do, but I got the intuitive nudge that it would be our best option (more on trusting your gut in Step 3).

On the drive over, my daughter and I played future-casting to clear out all the things I didn't want to happen when we got there. "Remember when we went to the Walmart vet, and there was absolutely no wait?" I said to her.

"Oh yeah, that was so great."

"And remember how they were so nice? And took such great care of our kitties? They were able to help them right away and get them exactly what they needed to get better?"

"Yes, that was amazing," my daughter agreed.

Guess what? We got exactly what I futurecasted. On a Saturday afternoon, the sparkling clean friendly clinic was completely empty. We had all four of their staff members giving our kitties their full attention, and we left with medicine, supplements, and all the advice we needed to take care of them. It was truly a five-star experience, transformed from what could very well have been a total shit-show. I caught myself in time, flipped the energy, and told the Universe how I wanted to be treated. Yes, like a freaking queen, thank you very much!

One of the reasons futurecasting works so well is that talking about your desires as if they already manifested puts you in a state of gratitude and celebration for the thing you want rather than judgment of what hasn't shown up yet.

Another reason is because it engages what philosopher Nevile Goddard coined the *Law of Assumption.*

Law of Assumption

Law of Assumption is a different spin on Law of Attraction. Law of Attraction says you attract that to which you're a vibrational match. Your thoughts and feelings will influence what shows up in your life. However, when you're using the Law of Attraction to manifest what you desire, you're functioning from a place of not having what you want and needing to "attract" it. With the Law of Assumption, you instead assume you already have it, or that it's already on its way to you.

Romance author Molly O'Hare used this powerful tool to hit the *USA Today* bestseller list with her book *Learning Curves.* She affirmed to herself over and over during the week: "I assume I've hit the list."

Note how different that is from "I want to hit the *USA Today* list," or worse, "Some day, I'll hit the list."

Please, please, please, keep things out of the "some day" realm. While it sounds like you're asking the Universe for something to show up in your future, you're actually pushing it away by filing it in the hopes and dreams category. You don't really believe it will show up. It's like the old, "one day when my ship comes in" feeling. Using future casting or Law of Assumption works far more effectively to call to you what you desire.

Try using the word "assume" with all your requests, like:

- I assume a parking space will be right there in front for me when I arrive.
- I assume I will make six figures this year.
- I assume I will find the perfect pair of shoes when I go shopping.
- I assume I will finish this manuscript ahead of schedule.
- I assume readers will adore my book.
- I assume I will go viral on Tiktok.

If you had a hard time saying "I assume readers will adore my book" because you think it sounds too arrogant, this is a clue that you have more to clear in the area of worthiness and being willing to be successful. Think about it–if you're shooting for six figures this year, then having readers who adore your books are part of that package. Go back to Step 1 and clear, clear, clear all those limiting beliefs until you can say it without choking, stuttering, or laughing!

We'll talk more about living, breathing, and embodying the energy of your future in Step 5: Live it Now.

Case Study: Alicia Rades - Law of Assumption

Alicia Rades is a *USA Today* bestselling author of young adult and new adult paranormal fiction. She learned about manifesting in 2018 from hearing other authors talk about it and has been working with it ever since. "I'm just learning–it's all starting to click," she said. She and her co-author discuss and use it all the time. "We'll call each other up to say, *I'm having trouble with this thing, let's talk about manifesting.*"

She and her coauthor set the intention to manifest an audio contract with a traditional publisher. "It was more vanity–we wanted someone to tell us we were good enough to have an audio contract." Within a few months, a publisher contacted them, and they signed a three-book contract.

Over the following year, they realized their self-published audios were far more lucrative. "We wanted to get control over this again and chose to manifest our rights back. We were told this was not possible, but we contacted the company anyway, using the Law of Assumption and trusting we would reach an agreement. It took six months of negotiating with them. They said they didn't do it, but we kept emailing. They quoted us a total of $16,000.00 in fees. We didn't know how we would get the money, as this was several months' worth of income at the time. However, we trusted the money would come."

Alicia said magically, miraculously, a series of grants, refunds, and other income appeared for them. "Six weeks later, we'd already manifested the funds—all because we made the assumption we'd get it."

The pair went from making roughly $100 per month off those three audiobooks to making multiple four figures per month consistently after self-publishing. "We learned that if your original manifestation isn't suiting you, you can change or enhance it to get the desired results."

Alicia said, "Boiling it down, I think the biggest thing is to believe in yourself and the process. That's where I stumbled most and where all the magic happens. There are two things I've been journaling about lately—one is the affirmation that I belong. I belong wherever I want to be. If I want to have millions of dollars in audio, I need to believe I belong in the room with people already achieving that, speaking on stage with those people."

The other phrase she's been journaling is *It is happening*. "I could never get into the *It has already happened* in 3D because my brain couldn't wrap around that. I don't have a million-dollar career in the 3D yet, but I've written the books and the Universe is arranging things for me. ***It is happening***." With the Law of Assumption, the statement *It is happening* is a true statement. We may or may not know the ways in which the Universe is conspiring to align, and we don't have to know the details—*It is happening* though. Our role is to allow it to and trust it will happen.

Freewriting: Tap into Your Genius

- Where do you want to be as an author in three years?
- Put yourself there—imagine it's already happened. What does your life look like?
- What are you doing differently? Better?
- Is that something you can already integrate today?
- What is one thing you could do immediately that would improve your career?
- What's the next step for you in your writing career?
- What blocks you from being the brilliant millionaire author that you are?

Chapter 7

Harnessing the Power of Inspiration

T o keep inspiration fresh and in front of you every day, you'll want to surround yourself with your vision of your highest life. Approach this playfully—have fun. Follow what's joyful for you. The following are some ideas for keeping the dream bright and in focus. They aren't requirements to manifesting your desires–your intention alone is powerful enough–but they help you maintain clarity about where you're headed. Making a game out of playing with the energies keeps you in the right headspace, and by surrounding yourself with your inspiration, it can soak in on subconscious levels.

Make a dream board or other visual inspiration

A dream board that you see every day reminds you of your intentions and targets. Some people use Pinterest or a digital art program like Picmonkey to make their inspiration boards.

I know for me, I sometimes stop seeing things around

me when they've been there for a while. I'll make a dream board in January, and within a few months, I fail to notice it anymore. You can move it around the house, so it will catch your eye again, or refresh it every few months with new pictures or inspiration. Afterall, it's working its magic, and you're getting clearer and clearer. So continue dreaming throughout the year as the inspiration flows.

This year, I went to a more simple bullet list of things I want to manifest to keep me focused. I'm playing with the list, moving things around, adding, subtracting as I'm inspired when I check in with my gut each day.

Making a dream board can be as easy as having a bulletin board by your writing desk where you pin things up to inspire you. I make dream boards the same way I freewrite–I try to tap into my subconscious and eliminate the editor or conscious mind, so I can bring forth the real essence of my intentions. Making dream boards is a great activity to do with a friend or a group of friends. I often invite my author friends over at the beginning of January, so we can make them together.

If you want to channel some magic into making a physical dream board, try this fun method.

Materials:

- Poster board or foam core
- Gluestick & scissors
- Stacks of magazines, old calendars, things with pictures that make you happy
- Stickers, scrapbook materials (if desired)

- Photoshop of an interview with yourself on the front page of the Sunday *New York Times* book review section or whatever is fun for you
- Screenshot your BookReport royalties but change it to make it the end of the year and add zeros, so it is huge.
- Photoshop one of your book covers onto the top charts
- Print-out of words or photos you might not easily find in magazines that relate to specifics goals, like:
- The *USA Today* Bestseller List logo
- the *New York Times* #1
- Intentions for the year
- "Fandemonium"
- "$5 Million in royalties"
- "My books went viral on Tiktok."
- "In 2023, I'm so grateful for...."
- Remember to dream about how you want to live your life too. What are you going to do with that $5 Million? Where will you live? What's your lifestyle? Are you traveling? Where to?

1) **Gather all your materials** before you begin and place them in the center of the table where you're working.

2) **Set a timer for thirty minutes to collect pictures.** Bring that same mindset you use in freewriting–don't stop to think, just keep moving as you go through the

magazines or old calendars and rip out any pictures that feel yummy to you or represent the energy of what you're going for. For example, if a beach vacation makes you feel abundant, rip out pictures of beaches and glorious turquoise water. The timer gives you that "sprint" mentality. This isn't the time to edit or plan, just rip out as many as you can find that represent the future you're creating. It's also not the time to use the scissors and cut things out perfectly. Just tear and go.

If you're working in a group, let your friends know the kinds of things you're looking for, so they can rip them out and pass them over when they come across one. For example, if the owl is your spirit guide, you might ask for someone to rip out any owls. Obviously in our profession, stacks of books or headlines about books being made into movies are great.

3) **Assemble the dream board.** At the end of the thirty minutes, you should have a stack of possible pictures. Sort through them to pick out your favorites. Big colorful pictures (like the ocean or a big flower) might make better backgrounds to paste smaller words or specific images onto. Be creative. Remember, you don't have to stay within the lines of the posterboard. I sometimes paste a uniquely shaped cut-out on the side of my board, so part of it extends beyond the natural edge. I've also seen people go 3-D, crumpling pictures to give them texture and make them stand up in relief on their boards. Sometimes, I'll set a timer for 30-45 minutes at this stage, too, because it helps everyone stay out of the editor's mind and in the realm of intuitive choosing.

. . .

4). **Know when to stop.** Like learning when to leave the party or to stop drinking, you should be aware of when there's too much of a good thing. If your board gets too cluttered, your eye may not be able to focus and rest on the things you intend to inspire you. Don't keep adding, even if you still have a pile of pictures beside you. The point isn't to get every picture pasted on, it's to have visual inspiration you like to look at on a daily basis. You're looking for the energy of what you want to call into your life. The pictures don't have to be perfect or your exact dream.

5). **Energize it.** If you're working in a group, have each person go around and share the highlights of their board. You can send your intention out into the Universe with words like "I'll have this or something better." Then be sure to clear anything that might prevent you from receiving everything on your board by saying something like "Anything that doesn't allow me to receive everything on this board, I now clear throughout all levels, layers, time, and dimensions."

Reminders and Prompts

You want to keep your eyes on the prize. This means having reminders around you every day of what you're calling into your life. This will help you change your abundance set point. If you constantly see your BookReport showing an extra zero, you will become desensitized to that large of a number and learn to expect the Universe to deliver it.

In addition to the dream board, you could do things like:

- Change all your passwords to something like "7-Fig-Author" or "Millionaire-Author" or simply "I-am-abundant"
- Label your bank account with something fun like "7figs" or "My Millions". My savings account is called "Treasure Chest". When I was saving for a Tesla, I labeled it "New Tesla".
- Make your perfect Millionaire Author day a visualization you do for a few moments every morning because your brain cannot tell the difference between things that are real and things that are imagined.
- Better yet, treat yourself to that actual perfect Millionaire Author day! Book the spa day, check yourself into a hotel for uninterrupted writing time, have coffee delivered. Whatever it is that makes you feel like a millionaire!

I highly recommend my co-author H. L. Savino's book, *Your Journey Into Abundance: A 29 Day Program to Attract Wealth, Success and Serious Joy.* It is full of daily practices and games to play to keep yourself in the flow.

You Don't have to Worry About the "How"

We tend to limit ourselves with our fixed ideas about how things should be done or are going to work out. We come to conclusions based on what we've learned from the past instead of checking in with our gut or intuition. When we believe there's only one way to do something, one limited pathway to success, we collapse all the infinite pathways we might have used to get there instead.

Any time you've already projected how things are going to turn out, or decided that one certain thing has to happen in order for you to get the result you want, you severely limit the outcome. The Universe can't engage with all the magic available because you've already said no to those other avenues. You're sending the message that it can only send you abundance in the certain way you've decided you can receive it.

Imagine your house is at the center of a network of roads. Abundance could show up at your house from any of these roads, in any kind of vehicle, but you've decided it can only come in a yellow cab on Main Street. Now, the Universe has a lot less to work with to orchestrate this delivery of abundance! Maybe the Main Street yellow cabs only deliver once every five years, but if you allowed abundance from the other roads, you could get a delivery every five days.

Worrying about "how" you will hit your money target is not just unnecessary, it's detrimental to manifesting. That doesn't mean you should ignore and not act on intuitive nudges when they come, but we'll talk more about that in Step 4.

In 2019, I was so certain that if I could just master Facebook ads (even though I had already taken five classes on them and was quite competent), then I'd be a millionaire author. I got so caught up on it, I spent fifty percent more than the year before to make only an additional hundred thousand dollars and became increasingly frustrated. It was because I'd made the decision that Facebook ads were *the one and only answer to my abundance.* I cut myself off from other possibilities.

In fact, it turned out translations, not Facebook ads, were the thing that catapulted me into seven figures. Do I still use Facebook ads? Yes. Particularly for my translations!

When you try to control your career too closely, you shut down all the possibilities. Opening up to infinite possibilities for any situation expands your energy field and allows for quantum entanglements. The Universe can gift you everything you desire when you're open. It's when you worry about the "hows," when you decide what needs to happen, that you collapse the field and limit all the ways the Universe can step into to help.

Case Study: Tess Thompson - Clear Intentions

Tess Thompson is the *USA Today* Bestselling and award-winning author of contemporary and historical Romantic Women's Fiction with nearly forty published titles. She recently posted in the Author Abundance group that she'd just had the highest monthly revenue of her career.

> "Vision boards, manifesting, believing—it works!" she wrote in her post.

Tess attributes her success to setting clear, purposeful intentions and then focusing on them. "Once you know what you want, everything you do has intention, which leads to the outcome you want. I believe there are a lot of things we don't understand about the Universe and the way things work."

Her goal was to hit seven figures from her author business this year and make an all-star bonus in KU, which she has already achieved. "I have all these stickers and post-it notes in my office and around the house with the revenue numbers I want. When I open my make-up drawer there is a sticky note with the number $2740, which is the amount you have to earn per day to hit a million for the year.

"The first day I hit that exact number, I showed it my husband and said *this is so weird!*"

Tess said it took a year, but she kept believing it would happen, especially during the setbacks. "It's the money blocks, you have to work through them. I swear it works. I don't understand how, but it does."

If the year continues as it has been, she's on target to hit that 7-figure goal this year. "I never thought it would be possible but things changed when my mindset did."

"It is possible to reach your dreams, even big fat lofty ones. It took time and effort but most of all, belief in myself and my stories. Seeing it happen to some of the ladies in the [Author Abundance Facebook] group has inspired me beyond measure. I hope my post will do the same for anyone feeling discouraged. I've been there. Just keep believing!! You will get there!"

In addition to setting clear goals, Tess also uses the other steps in this book, including loving her books and trusting her gut.

Despite the fact that "Everyone says don't write clean or historical because there's no money in it," Tess writes both because that's what she loves.

"I had this idea for a historical series, it came to me in a dream. I was in the middle of a long contemporary series, but I wrote it down. Two years later, I pulled out the notebook and reread it. I gave the series to myself as a Christmas gift–I allowed myself to write what I wanted to for the month of December." The love Tess poured into the series paid off. "That series has totally taken off."

"We're always trying to fit in or go with the trends, not

that writing to market is a bad thing, but you have to find your own magic and go with that.

I think whatever it is that makes you unique–lean into it."

— *Tess Thompson*

Step 3: Love Your Books

Chapter 8

Love is the Answer

Any time I'm asked to give advice to authors, my number one tip is always to "Love your books." It sounds so esoteric, so impractical, and yet it is the energy that will make things happen for you.

When you think about it, it makes so much sense. When you love your book, you're going to enjoy working on it. You're going to find the best cover for it. You're going to spend time working with a beta reader and editor. You're going to format it properly and make it beautiful. If you feel the urge to market the book, you're going to invest in it. When you love your books, it's so simple and you easily find the way forward.

Whenever I get stuck in my writing, my instinct is to tear apart the manuscript and my ideas—to start judging either the book or myself as a writer. This is not an energy that creates; it's an energy that destroys. I don't know about you, but the more judgmental I get of my book, the more lost I become. Like a half-knit sweater, the more I tug on certain threads, the whole thing starts to unravel until I don't know top from bottom—what works, what doesn't.

How do you talk to yourself about your books when you're feeling this way? Do any of these sound familiar?

- I don't know what's happening.
- Is this plot too boring?
- Is my hero too much of an asshole?
- Is my hero too soft / beta?
- Is my character too dumb to live?
- Are the descriptions too dull?
- I'll never write as well as X author.
- The writing isn't as good as my past book.
- This isn't real literature.
- Kissing books are just lady-porn.
- I'm so stuck.
- Is this funny / entertaining /scary enough?
- Does anyone want to read this stuff?
- Is this just like a million other books in my genre?
- Will anyone ever care about this book besides me and my mother/sister/bff/husband/partner?
- I can't figure out what comes next.
- I don't know what to do.

None of those questions or statements are going to help you find the answer.

Instead, flip the energy. Ask yourself,

- What did I love about this book when I started?

- What were the scenes that made me swoon / sweat / pee my pants with glee?
- Why do I love the characters / topic?
- Where are my favorite parts?
- Where was I enjoying myself when I wrote?

Just like in couples therapy, when the therapist starts by asking how you first fell in love, returning to that initial love, that spark, changes everything.

As soon as I'm back in the state of appreciation for my book, the answers start to flow again. I suddenly know where I'm going, or how to fix the thing that was throwing it off. When the judgment lifts away, it's easier to see what needs to happen. You'll trust your own instincts and get out of your own way and miracles will happen. Whether it's writing the book, fixing the plot, figuring out the launch, knowing how to tell readers about it, putting it on sale, getting it translated or narrated as an audiobook, your passion for your book will show the way.

Meditation: Love your Books

Use this meditation to connect with the energy of your books and surround them with love.

1. Close your eyes. Imagine your energy like a giant ball of light that extends three feet beyond you in every direction.
2. Expand your energy out a hundred million miles to encompass all that is.
3. Invite in the energy of a particular book, series, or your entire catalog.
4. Take a moment to just experience the energy of that book or series of books.
5. Send gratitude to your work. Thank it for being. Love it.
6. Ask it what it needs from you. (Often authors hear that it just needs more love or to be appreciated, but you may get a specific task or marketing idea)
7. Reverse the flow of energy and receive from your work. What does it want to gift to you?

How can it contribute to your life? Will you allow it to contribute?

8. Repeat steps five and seven, sending gratitude and receiving back from your book as many times as feels good or interesting to you. When you're finished, thank the book or books again before you disconnect from their energy, open your eyes and return to your day.

Case Study: Leigh James - Receiving, Hitting the USA Today list

Author Leigh James writes billionaire romance and young adult paranormal romance under the name Leigh Walker.

"I've been doing mindset work for four years. At some point, I started writing in a journal every day." She used a daily journal exercise of writing the things she was grateful for, ten dreams she'd already made happen, and the next goal she was going to achieve.

On July 22, 2020, she started writing, *I am a USA Today Bestselling Author* as her goal to achieve next. "I had just started to bring books wide and had never hit a list before, other than with a boxset." At the time, hitting the list was a reach goal considering where her sales were. Still, she wrote it down every single day for a month straight.

"I finished my journal and forgot about it. I started working on a different goal."

Around the same time, she joined our Author Abundance monthly membership. She loved finding a group of authors who felt the same way. "You can feel the energy. You've shown me something and taught me something that I didn't know was possible over a Zoom call–it's been life-changing." She also started working with my co-author Lee Savino for private mindset coaching.

In February 2021, she published her books on reading apps like Radish and KISS. In the process of loading her book by chapter onto Radish, she had to reread it. "I reread my book *Escorting the Billionaire*, which I'd published five years earlier." As she went through it, she fell in love with it again. It had done well in Kindle Unlimited when she released it originally, and she had the thought that if she'd released wide, it probably could have hit the *USA Today* list.

"Unbeknownst to me, KISS started running a massive Facebook ad campaign for this book. I went on Amazon, and there was a huge spike in my sales. I didn't know what happened. I started getting emails from people." She'd nearly let the Leigh James penname die at that point–she no longer had a mailing list and had gone to a free Wix website. "I was getting messages. People said they saw the ad and couldn't stop reading. I thought I was being targeted by bots or something negative."

Over the next week, readers went bananas. "I sold 9,000 copies of a five-year-old full-priced book. It hit the *USA Today* two weeks in a row–out of nowhere. It was a *God moment* to me. It was amazing. I was feeling positive energy from the abundance group, and this happened out of the blue."

As you might imagine, her income multiplied as well. She went from fluctuating between five and six figures a year to nearly hitting seven figures. "Now it's come back to earth, and I need to get back into my mindset. I need to focus because it works."

One of the key mindset elements for her was believing

she was enough. "The actual belief that I was good enough, that I was worthy, those things operated in tandem."

"I've seen such significant changes in my life since changing my mindset.

— *Leigh James*

This works. Be diligent and vigilant with yourself. If you're committed to the practice–seeing the good in yourself and the world–that goodness comes back to you."

Chapter 9

Flipping Your Self-Talk

Just like flipping scripts for your money wounds, flipping your self-talk from criticism to admiration can transform your entire life.

We have this fear that if we don't constantly put our lives, our work, our actions under a microscope to make sure we did everything right, we're going to become egotistical. In fact, I believe the opposite is true.

Often the place you judge yourself the most is the area you have the most potential.

When I first started teaching modern dance to adults, it wasn't because I thought I was so great and had a lot to offer. The current teacher was leaving and asked me to step in. Even though I'd been dancing for twenty years, I didn't have a degree in dance, so I felt "less-than" as a teacher.

Terrified of not getting it right, wanting to be liked by

my students, and the need to "perform" rather than be present made me rigid in how I constructed my class. I modeled it strictly after the structure of the departing teacher's class and reused / recycled most of her material.

My doubt in my own abilities to come up with something new or creative completely stifled my process. Did people keep coming? Did they like me? Yes. It worked. But it could have been so much more.

In *Manifest Your Destiny*, Wayne Dyer described his worry before he gave a talk about whether people would like him and how he learned to change it into the question, "how can I serve?" It made a huge difference for him in terms of the words and the energy he imparted while speaking.

When I went into teaching my dance class with that mentality, what came out was less praise for my students and more pointed feedback. After class I said to my friend, "I feel like I was a bitch in that class." She told me it was the best one I'd ever taught.

My fears had been shutting me down.

I just needed a huge dose of ego sauce poured on my head about my ability to teach.

I did have the answers, I did know how to give more, but I was holding myself back out of fear of getting it wrong and people not liking me.

Where do you criticize yourself most? What if that was actually your greatest gift or capacity? I know that sounds strange, but stay with me here.

One of the places I criticize myself most for is being disorganized. If I took a photo of my desk right now and included it in this book, you'd wonder how I even function.

If I showed you how many tabs I have open on my computer while I write this, you'd snicker. It's ridiculous! And yet... if I pour some ego sauce on this trait of mine and look for the gifts...wow. Actually, my ability to function in a state of chaos is a gift. I am highly flexible. I can write anywhere–in the car, at Starbucks, at my kid's swim lesson. I can write three books at once. I can help two kids home school during quarantine without slowing my output.

That's not your gift? That's okay! What is?

Look to the places where you judge yourself most, pour some ego sauce on it to flip your limiting beliefs, and uncover how that is actually one of your greatest strengths.

So back to books. When you pour this ego sauce onto yourself as a writer and your books, you'll find your strengths. You'll know how to market your book better. Instead of working hard to fit in or follow the lines set by other authors who you perceive as successful, you'll expand into the spaces you excel and write more of what you love.

I remember as a new parent, one of those ever-debated topics was how much to hold your baby. One of the moms in my group declared with total certainty, "You can't spoil a baby with love."

I had to stop and think about it because that's another one of those ideas that gets ingrained from society. Children get "spoiled" by kindness. By nurturing. By acceptance. Instead, we were supposed to point out all their flaws and slap their hands and show them everything they've done wrong, so they will turn out right.

Hmm.

How well does that work?

Sure, flowers can still bloom under harsh conditions, but wouldn't they do better with plenty of light, water, and proper soil?

Don't be afraid that you will spoil your book—okay, not your book, but yourself as the author—by pouring ego sauce all over your project. Steep in it awhile. Find out what you love about your book; it won't make you oblivious to what's not working. In fact, it will be the opposite. You'll know what tweaks are necessary to make it better (not to fix it!). When you stop operating from judgment and criticism, you're far more able to see how to improve.

Being in an energy of love will in turn make your readers love the book. When you pour love into your book, they can feel it when they read it. When you love your characters, you write them better. When you delight yourself with plot twists, the readers will be delighted!

Energetically speaking, you will receive the energy that matches. **So if you love your book, readers will also love it.** If you hate on your book...

Let's not even go there.

You don't want to embed the energy of your criticism into your book, or you'll end up with critical readers and bad reviews.

Even if the book is already written, published, and on the market, pouring your love into it still works. *It will sell your books!*

I have a few fun stories about this. In the summer of 2020, my co-author, Lee Savino, was doing a few Facebook live videos for her fans from her business page. She went to her bookshelf to select one of her books to read out loud and randomly chose our co-written book, *Alpha's Prey*, which had been written and published over a year before.

She started reading it to find a passage to read to her fans and as she did, she fell back in love with the book. She found it hard to choose just one passage to share. When she read the passage to her fans, it was hard to stop reading. She felt like she could have read the entire book! Later that week, on a whim, she applied for a Bookbub on the book. Lo and behold, it got accepted right away!

This happened again in December 2020. Our co-written book *Alpha's War* was about to be published in German, so Lee had just emailed me the new translated cover.

"He's so hot," I said to her, admiring our cover model when I opened the email.

"You know, you're right," Lee said and—remembering how well it worked to apply while she was in that space of appreciation—once again applied for a Bookbub on the book. At the time, Lee had been rejected for several Book-bubs in a row. (Whenever you get a rejection email, just apply again, or better yet, get yourself into a space of appre-ciation for your book and *then* apply). That week she applied for *Alpha's War,* and again the book I had just given love to was immediately selected for a Bookbub.

One of my favorite stories about seeing love for a book make an otherwise inexplicable difference was in audio-books. I had just started publishing them and found that listening to them at the checkpoint was cringy and awkward —especially the sexy bits. I often even skipped and skimmed through them.

This particular time, however, I had a nine-hour road-trip to make, so I decided to give this book—the second in a Regency series—a listen. As I reviewed, I fell in love with the book again. I had that experience you've probably all had of remembering everything I originally loved about it while writing it. Yes, I still cringed a little during the sex scenes, but otherwise, it made for the most enjoyable ride ever. I approved the audio, and it went live.

Many months later, I was reviewing my sales on ACX and discovered that one particular audiobook had triple the number of sales of the other two books in the series–the one I'd listened to and showered with my love! I checked to see if I'd put it in a different category or to find out if anything different had happened, but no. There was no difference. And there wasn't anything else special about the book. The ebook had certainly not sold better than the others in the series. In fact, it had sold fewer copies. There was nothing logical to explain the increased sales other than my energy of total love for the book when I approved it for sale!

Try pouring love into your project. Trying pouring ego sauce over your own head as you write it. See if, in fact, rather than you becoming an egotistical monster who can't see how bad you are, you don't expand your writing abilities, getting deeper into your story or craft, finding more flow, and expanding the possibilities for your manuscript.

Love is the magic that makes it all work.

Case Study: Mary E. Thompson – Loving Your Book

USA Today Bestselling Author Mary E. Thompson has been writing contemporary and romantic suspense for almost nine years.

She joined the Author Abundance Facebook group not long after it was formed. "I am quiet, so I didn't jump in a lot, but I was reading posts and definitely thinking about my mindset." She signed up for the monthly membership when it began. "I didn't make all the calls and still don't get to all of them live, but when I go, I always leave feeling like my world is shifting."

In late December 2021, she decided to make a first-in-series book free. "I knew the book was good and had been pouring my love into it for months after the calls and really changing my mindset."

She said she was always a *write it and move on* kind of person, but after the calls, knew she had to remind herself how much she loved each and every book when she was writing it. "This book was special. At the time it was released, I had my highest number of preorders. Almost two years after release, when I decided to move it to permafree, I knew the book deserved a big splash, so I applied for a Bookbub Featured Deal."

She was producing an audiobook for the same book around the same time, so she had to go back through it and reread it. "I'm a #6 futuristic [in the Strengthsfinder personality assessment], so as soon as it's done, I move on. Even during editing, I'm ready to go to the next book." As she went through the audiobook, she fell back in love with the book. "I thought, this is such a good story, I really like these characters, it came together. It felt right that it was the one I could get the free Bookbub for."

Although she'd received a handful of international-only Bookbub Featured Deals, she had never received a free one in the US and only had one that included the US. She was delighted when the new permafree book was accepted for a featured deal for January 2022.

"I was shocked, but I went into it knowing it would be amazing. I downloaded the other freebies that week to support the other authors celebrating a Bookbub Featured Deal with me, and I applied for another one." Once more, she was delighted to get one for a month after the first one ran.

"This one was for a $0.99 single title book. My bestselling book from an older series. Again, I knew it was going to be amazing, and it was." After that one, she applied yet again. She received a few rejections, but didn't give up because she knew her books deserved the recognition. "Less than two weeks after my second Bookbub Featured Deal of 2022, I got accepted for a third one! My acceptance came less than 12 hours after I submitted it, for another permafree book that had been permafree for 5 years! It was another book that I knew deserved love, and because of Author Abundance Mindset, I was giving the book that love, and the Universe plucked it out and showed the world."

Mary said, "In the first five months of 2022, I've earned more than all of 2021." She hasn't received her fourth Bookbub Featured Deal yet, but she is certain she will get another one this year. "In fact, I know I'll get three more this year. I'm going to bring home more money this year than my husband, and I'm going to make our lives everything we dream they can be."

She said, "I really appreciate your help making that happen. I wanted to thank you for sharing your knowledge with me and for writing your book because I know it's going to change my life even more. Thank you for that!"

Mary is now a firm believer in loving her books. Her advice to other authors: "Surround yourself with your books. They're in our heads, but we need to remind ourselves of them."

"I'm in my basement and don't have finished walls, but one thing I've always wanted to do is have my book covers on the walls around me. I have sixty-six books published. If I wallpapered my office with my book covers, it would be much more of a reminder of everything I've done for nine years."

Freewriting: Tap into your Intuition

Freewrite until nothing else comes out to answer the following prompts:

- What are the three (or more) areas I judge myself most?
- If I pour ego sauce on it, what potential lies in those areas? What are the gifts I'm hiding from myself?
- What do I love about my book or books?
- What do I do well as a writer?
- What do my books want me to know?

When I ask this question, the hero of my book often talks to me, reassuring me that the book is going to be loved, or I'm shown a scene that's missing.

- How can I receive more from my books?

You might not get words to write down from this prompt. Rather, it could show up as more of an energetic receiving than anything words can express. Just open up your aware-ness to whatever comes. Whether it's just a feel-good or the energy of the book, take it in.

- What am I grateful for in my author career?
- Which people are a gift or contribution to my career?

Even just asking this question invites more helpful people into your world.

Step 4: Trust Your Gut

Chapter 10

Only You Have the Answer

No one has the answers for your career but you.

It took me a long time to trust that. I took all the courses, followed all the advice. But the truth is, we can't replicate anyone else's success. I object to the idea that someone else holds the answer, and if I just follow their lead, I'll have the same results. That's not how life works. It's not how energy works.

Again—I can't say it enough—*no one else holds the answers to my success.*

Think about the ever-present debate of Kindle Unlimited vs. Wide. If there was a clear answer that one direction was right and the other was wrong, *there wouldn't be a debate.* People in both camps are making boatloads of money. You don't have to pin your success on this one particular decision. Rather, you learn to trust your own gut, which involves your own perfect timing, for absolutely every decision you make for your books.

There's no need to crowd-source decisions like:

- Traditionally publish or go indie

- Put your books into Kindle Unlimited or publish wide
- Rapid release or use a relaxed publishing schedule
- Hire a translator or sell your foreign rights

You can ask for advice and input, of course, but I'm not even advocating that you make these decisions from logic.

I'm suggesting you make them from your gut. And don't think that once you've made a decision, it's the end-all answer. Things change and evolve. What works for one book might not work for the next. The market shifts, tastes shift. Your writing may shift. Maybe trad publishing was perfect for you, but you're getting the nudge to try indie. Maybe you're getting the nudge to go trad. In this chapter, I will teach you how to tap into your own sense of knowing to find the answer to every question.

Your intuitive hits are money

Pay attention to the ideas that seemingly "drop" into your head—they weren't connected to the thoughts you were having. That's intuition talking. **Those ideas are money.**

You can follow a formula and have it work, but ultimately, being open to and acting on divine inspiration creates things you never could have predicted–amazing things. Be careful that you don't refuse to change course after your gut led you to one success. Truth is in the moment with each book. We have to keep checking in with our inner guidance, keep asking questions and staying open to the answers at every turn.

One of the early moments in my career when I had one

of these ideas drop into my head out of nowhere was when I wrote my first shifter romance *The Alpha's Hunger*. For one thing, I had planned to give it to one publisher, but as I was finishing it, I felt strongly that it needed to go to a different one. Then, the moment I finished the book, I had a nudge to write a short bonus story to go with the book and offer it for free as a means of selling the full-priced book. I trusted the guidance. I knew this wasn't an idea I'd come up with on my own through reasoning or someone's suggestion, it had just dropped into my head without being connected to any previous thoughts. I wrote the bonus story, and my publisher put it up for free at the same time they published the book. It worked like gangbusters. That book sold and sold. The freebie pushed the full-priced book, and it was one of my all-time bestsellers for several years.

Another time, I released my book *Alpha Bully*, with a cover that I'd talked myself into, thinking it was right for the book. Almost immediately after release, I had a strong notion that the cover needed to change. In the past, I'd sort of prided myself on not being a cover diva. One of those authors who gets fussy and demands change after change trying to get to some idea of perfect. As the former director of a dance company, I remembered how every dancer would always complain about the costumes the choreographer picked for them. I figured it was like that–authors never love their covers, but they just have to suck it up. But in this case, I was willing to pull a diva and call in the last minute change with the designer. As soon as I put on the new cover, the book started to sell, and this one also hit it out of the park.

Side note–I don't think you're a diva for wanting the perfect cover. I do think you should study the market and make sure your cover properly sells your book or...even better–use your inner knowing to make the decision.

But Renee, those golden ideas don't always drop into my head. How am I supposed to use my inner guidance?

Don't worry. I've got you.

The next chapter includes everything you need to access your intuition for any decision—small or large.

Tap into your inner guidance for *everything*

The main purpose of having this book as a workbook is to give you the opportunity to tap into your own knowing. I've found freewriting to be one of the easiest and most accessible ways to get intuitive answers, which is why I've included the journal prompts.

My good friend and quantum healer, Simone Gers, has trained herself to check her gut and follow the guidance she receives on even the smallest things. She asks what clothes to wear each morning, what her body wants to eat, etc. She's often surprised by the answer only to understand later why she received that guidance. For example, she'll be drawn to wear a sweater on what seems like a warm day, and then the weather will take a sudden turn.

One day she had a huge stack of work to do and none of it felt fun. Feeling overwhelmed, she asked the Universe, "what do I need to get this all done?" Surprisingly, the answer she heard was, "Go see a funny movie."

Of course, her response was, "Excuse me? I said I had a pile of work to do. I don't have time to drive into town and watch a movie."

But the prompting was clear, and she'd learned to trust her inner guidance. She abandoned her pile of papers to grade and long list of to dos and took herself to see a funny movie. As it turned out, it was such a nice relief from the work she had to do, that when she got home, several tasks were taken care of by the Universe—other people did them or they worked themselves out releasing her from a task— and she breezed through the remaining small pile of work in no time at all and with far more joy and energy than she would've had if she'd stayed home to put her nose to the grindstone.

We'll talk more about getting support from the Universe when you're overwhelmed or burned out at the end of the book, but the message here is that **asking a question will always yield the right answer.**

Go Against the Grain

One place I've trusted my gut contrary to popular advice is by breaking the "stay in your lane" law as an author. You've heard the advice–figure out your branding and stick to it. Don't write outside the tropes or lines of your genre, or if you do, pick a new pen name. There are lots of good reasons for this. Branding is the obvious one. Training the algorithms to show your books is another one.

But that's not how I roll. I write in several different romance genres. I have a series in paranormal romance, sci-fi romance, and dark romance. I even have older books in Regency and medieval romance. I don't use a separate pen name for each of them. I didn't use a separate pen name for this book although it probably would've made sense from an algorithm perspective. Some may think I'm lazy. And it's true—I didn't want to have to maintain more than one pen name. But I'm also connected to my intuition, which guided me to understand that one pen name was the way to move forward (at least up until now), and my readers would follow me from one genre to another, and for the most part, they do. It has worked for me. I trusted my gut rather than conventional wisdom. I follow my bliss as a writer, love the books I write, and it works even though it skews my branding.

Here's the biggest hint I can give you for authoring. There is no right or wrong. There's no one way to do things. There isn't one answer. You need to tune in and listen to what's right for you. Follow your gut.

When *USA Today* bestselling author Lisa Daily released her first book, a dating advice book, she planned to self-publish it, as she already worked in advertising and knew how to market it. It was her first book and her first experience publishing, so her energy was wide open to the possibilities, and magic happened. First, an agent who was friends with her publicist read the book and wanted to represent Lisa. Then, because Lisa had been invited to talk on the *Sally Jessy Raphael* show in New York, her agent scrambled to get her meetings with all the top six publishing houses. They met with the publishers, and she received offers from all six. She had to trust her gut on which one to take–the lower offer with a particularly savvy editor or higher offers from other firms. She trusted her gut and her agent's advice and went with the lower offer with the editor who was a mover and shaker. As it turned out, the editor wanted to "crash the book," which means get it out to market on an abbreviated schedule, in just a matter of weeks, so they could capitalize on Lisa's upcoming television appearance.

The book was in the stores in just six weeks–a feat that is simply unheard of in traditional publishing. It coincided with the release of the Sally Jessy Raphael appearance and sold like gangbusters. Truly, the Universe had her back at every turn.

Was every subsequent book release magical for Lisa? No. Like many authors, the first time can be the easiest, it's once we think we know how things will go that we shut down possibilities instead of being open to the energy of each moment.

Act swiftly

I've found there's a window of opportunity for all things. That's even more true with intuitive nudges, which is all the more reason to pay attention to them when they show up.

When you have one of those ideas that just drops into your head out of nowhere (not connected to any previous thoughts), write it down if you can.

For me, ideas often hit when I'm driving in my car or standing in the shower, which aren't great times to grab a pen and paper, but I do make it a practice to take heed and act swiftly. For example, if you get the idea to put a book on sale, schedule it right away, don't file it away in the back of your head as a good idea for "some time." Better yet, do a gut check. (See the next chapter for how-to's on *when* to schedule the sale). There might be an optimal day.

In our Author Abundance monthly membership group, I led a guided meditation for going viral on Tiktok. One of the things that came through in the meditation was to use your intuition with Tiktok. To stay open to the ideas for videos when they download, and then to post them immediately, following the energy of when is the best time to post for the algorithm. After many people on the call posted staggering results, I put it into practice myself and found that when I followed my gut about timing or content, the posts did far better than when I did what I thought was "supposed to do" on Tiktok (post three times a day, blah, blah, blah).

During the 2020 pandemic, my co-author Lee Savino didn't want to buy into the despair and lack mentality that had collapsed around our society. She actively worked on dwelling in an abundance mindset. She felt excited for the future despite all the news warnings and the crisis happening around the world. Prompted by an inner nudge–one of those ideas that dropped into her head–she called me up and said, "I think we should give away our books for free."

I interpreted that the way I wanted to hear it and responded, "Yes, good idea. Let's give away one of our books."

"No, not one. All of them."

I spun in a circle for just a few seconds. I mean...*all of our books?* Isn't that, um, a *few* too many?

But I could sense the abundance in her desire. She wasn't functioning from lack. She was in a space of generosity and love. She wanted to give back to the community. We weren't nurses or doctors. We couldn't help our neighbors that way. But we did have books. We could give people something to read while they were stuck at home in quarantine. And no, she didn't want to charge them a dime.

Gulp.

"Are you sure?" I asked.

"Yes. I want to put them all up for free," she insisted.

Knowing that her energy was in a far higher vibration than my own at that moment, I trusted her impulse.

We set up the sale for early April and watched in awe as there were over 150,000 downloads. The series had been earning less than $10,000 a month, and those numbers had been trending downward towards $5,000 a month in the months prior. In the month of April 2020, the series income shot up to $32,000, even though we had given away all eight books for free. It continued at that high level for three months and then very gradually declined.

"I don't even understand how that works," Lee said. "We gave away the books for free, but we gave with a grateful heart, and we received several times more than we gave." The books have been selling well ever since.

Recently I decided to put the first four books of an older series for free for a week to stimulate sales and the algorithms. I tried to get a Bookbub and Barnes and Noble promotion on book one, but in both cases was rejected. Then I heard (I tend to experience intuition as **clairaudience**–words in my head) to wait until Friday and then submit book four. I did, and received both promotions.

I mentioned clairaudience. That's just the way I tend to receive my intuitive hits, but they may show up for you as sensations, visions, scents, feelings, or just a calm, clear knowing. Intuition never comes with an emotion attached like fear so don't worry. If you're an anxious person like me and your thoughts spiral into *oh my God I have encephalitis!* (that has really happened in my head), that's not your gut talking. That's fear showing up to distract you from creating your future.

What I'm talking about is subtle. It's feeling like turn left here instead of taking the right you always take. It's the *walk into this store* nudge, when your mind is demanding you get home quickly. It's the flash of something unexpected and out of the normal for you and then acting on that impulse.

Many people are afraid of tapping into the unknown. They fear the information that might show up. The truth is, having answers from within is never a scary thing. I experience (note that I didn't say "I have" –because I don't want to affirm that it's mine or belongs to me) rheumatoid arthritis that causes conjunctivitis in my eyes during a flare up. My coach gave me the prompt: *what am I seeing that I don't want to see?* so I often use that as a freewriting prompt when I journal.

One day while using that prompt I heard, *your father is dying.* I was certainly grieved by the information. My dad had looked aged at Thanksgiving, but my conscious mind had not accepted the fact that he might not be well. Within two months of that intuitive hit, his doctor gave him the information that his lymphoma had become active. Two more months, and he passed.

Because I knew it was coming, I was able to move through and process his death with so much more grace than would have been possible if I hadn't had the information in advance of his rather quick departure.

I hope that story didn't scare you. I'm not saying that you will receive information about someone's death. But I related that story because that information, while not good news, gave me strength and quietude for the journey. Receiving answers creates a calm, settled feeling, not a frightening one.

So often the answers are there, available to us if we'd just ask the question. Possibly if I'd started with a question like "Is this the right book to submit? Or Is this the right time to submit?" *before* I first submitted, I could have avoided the rejections in the first place, but I didn't think to ask until I'd received the disappointing news.

Remember (this is a reminder to myself, as well!) that every book is different. Every week on Amazon or other retailers is different. You're a different person this month than you were last release. So you have to really tune in. Keep asking questions.

I always use intuition when invited to anthologies and other kinds of publications rather than logic or time schedule. I'll ask, *is this in my highest good? Will this create more?* If I get the answer that it does, I tweak my schedule and figure it out to make it work. I've also experienced that when I initially checked in, it was in my highest good and would create more, but somewhere along the way, it got heavy. So I checked in again. I had the courage to pivot when something was no longer in my highest good.

Case Study: Megan Linski – Following Intuition

Several years ago *USA Today* Bestselling Fantasy and Paranormal Author Megan Linski had one of those downloads from the Universe–the idea that drops into your head from nowhere. "I wrote it down on a piece of paper and forgot about it. A few weeks later, I saw a pre-made book cover that fit my idea perfectly. I bought the cover and wrote the book in less than two weeks, figuring it was a project just for fun, and I didn't really care if it sold or not."

"I genuinely wanted to do it. I didn't feel like I *had to* do it to make money or because it was what was hot right now. So many people will tell you you won't make money if you don't write in this trope at this second."

She didn't have any attachment to the book or the release. "I didn't have any resistance. I was merely curious about how it would perform and had a blast writing the story, which turned out to be far shorter than my more seriously written titles."

She knows that attachment to results can kill the energy of things. "Any time you have an air of desperation about something, it doesn't pan out," she said. "There's a difference between believing *failure's not an option* and *this has to succeed or else I'm doomed.* In one, you're manifesting success to come no matter what. In the other, you're clinging desperately to one outcome."

She released the book, spending less than $100 in advertisement for it and then ignored the project once again after she uploaded it for sale.

You already know how this is going to turn out, right? It has all the right pieces for magic to happen—a gut-inspired story, written for fun with no expectation.

Indeed, Megan said, "In the first three months of release, the book went viral, and I earned over $20,000 for it—more than I'd ever made on a release before and with less effort than I'd ever put into a project."

Was it luck? Or did Megan create that magic? "I definitely got lucky," she said, "but I think I manifested that luck and believe that following my intuition at the right time enabled me to be successful at the exact moment I needed to be."

Her advice to other authors is, "If there's an idea you have, don't try to resist it, just go for it. Trust your instincts. The biggest mistakes in my career have always been because I haven't trusted my instincts. I trusted what everyone else told me to do instead of doing what I needed to be doing."

She believes the biggest blocks and the longest paths we can take as authors are a result of listening to other people. "If I had done what I wanted to do years ago, I would be way farther ahead than I am right now."

She said, "You're put here to write the books you're meant to write. If you're writing the books everyone else is writing, it's not your purpose.

Only you can write the books you've been called to write.

— Megan Linski

If you're trying to be just like everyone else, and follow the trends, you'll never create the story you're destined for."

Freewriting: Tap into Your Genius

Think of the times you've trusted your gut (or not followed a gut instinct). What did it feel like? How did you know it was intuition talking and not fear or logic? Play with the following freewriting exercises to help tap into this powerful tool.

- Where do you not trust yourself?
- Where do you trust yourself?
- What intuitive hits have you had in the past?
- Where have you acted on intuition in your life?
- What method or methods of tapping into your inner knowing work best for you?
- When and where are you the most open to intuitive hits?

Chapter 11

Quick Guide to Accessing your Intuition

How do you trust your gut? There are many ways. In this book, we practice freewriting as the main one. I assume because you are writers, like me, putting a pen to the page will be as magical and illuminating for you as it is for me. Other methods may work well for you, too. The following is a quick guide to accessing your intuition. You can find the one that works best for you.

Journaling

I especially find early morning journaling to be particularly fruitful for receiving intuitive nuggets. I like to ask questions and then freewrite the answers. Keep your pen moving across the page without stopping or editing. You can prewrite your questions, use the many prompts in this book, or just do a question and answer as you go.

If you've read *The Artist's Way*, you may have already made a practice of what Julia Cameron calls "Morning Pages". When I first read the book and adopted this habit of freewriting five pages upon first waking every morning, it enabled me to use freewriting as a means to target my desires. I was working as a technical writer, and I manifested receiving (for my company, not for myself) a two million dollar grant. It did net me a little bonus and recognition, but the empowerment I received knowing I could write my way to my desires was invaluable.

Another added benefit of beginning the day by journaling is that when I've written my pages, I feel good about myself. I've invested in myself. Believed in myself. I'm inspired. I've set the tone for the day–I'm writing today! I've made time for me in my day. I'm important in my world. I'm courageous enough to contemplate, to uncover, to receive. And it feels good.

Type or handwrite your morning pages? Which will create something greater? Of course, feel into your knowing. I handwrite, and while I can type much faster and with so much more ease than sitting with pen and paper (My hand cramps when I really get going), what I've noticed is that there's a connection to my body and soul when I hold a pen in my hand that's magical. It's like my soul speaks through that connection. It's easy for me to get into flow state. The editor that cowrites with me at my keyboard doesn't show up for the pen and paper morning pages. Moving my hand across the paper, it's like my soul takes the wheel. It's an intimate act, and I feel connected. Powerful discoveries, ahas, gifts, come out on the page. For me, this practice is about presence—being present with my essence. Sometimes, I might go back and read something in a journal I'm currently working in because insights often come in bread crumbs, and it might be half a journal in before I realize oh, wow, that's big. While I don't often go back years later to reread past journals, I love having them in their special place, a reminder of my commitment to myself, my process, and my billionaire author life.

. . .

Light or Heavy

For this method, feel into the energy of the situation and then ask questions. For example, let's say you're wondering if you should promo stack with your Bookbub. You ask the question, should I promo stack? If it feels light and fluffy, it's a yes. If it feels heavy and dull, it's a no.

Muscle Testing

This method works well for yes or no questions. Make a ring between the thumb and pinkie of your non-dominant hand and then try to break the ring with the index finger of your dominant hand. If the ring holds strong, it's a yes; if it breaks, it's a no. This is only semi-reliable for me, but I think that's because sometimes the answer isn't a clear yes or no, it's more complicated than that. You may have to drill down and ask many yes or no questions to get clear.

Weigh Two Options

This only works with two options. Imagine you're holding one option in each hand and feel the energy in them. Which one feels brighter or bigger? For example, let's say you're choosing between two book covers. Hold your hands out like they're balancing scales and imagine one cover in your right hand and the other in your left. Which one tips the scale?

Look into the Future. Ask this question and either feel for the answer or freewrite/ journal the answer: "What would my life look like in six months (or one year, five years, etc) if I chose this?" FEEL or WRITE the answer. Then ask "What would my life look in ___ time if I didn't choose it?" and FEEL or WRITE the answer.

Pendulum

This is similar to muscle testing, but you can use it to pick between multiple options. I buy pendulums at the gem and mineral show in Tucson for three dollars, but if you don't want to buy one, you can use a nut or washer tied onto a piece of dental floss. it doesn't have to be fancy or a gemstone. You show the pendulum the different options as angles of the swing. For example, "Should I spend 10, 20, 30, 40 on this Facebook ad, or something different?" Each option is a different angle away from you. Then I close my eyes, so watching it won't influence the way it swings, set it off in a circle and wait until it settles into a swing. Then I open my eyes to see which direction it took.

I used that this morning to pick which air conditioner repairman to call. Once, when I bought property in Taos and had to get insurance, I pendulumed for which company to use. When a local asked me who I went with and I told them, they said, "Oh they're the best, how did you know that?" (Ancient Chinese secret. Wink.)

Pay attention to how something feels in your body

If none of the above ideas resonate for you, try just tuning into your body when thinking about a question. You've heard people talk about "gut instinct"? It's said that the gut is the "second brain" because it holds the enteric nervous system (ENS) with over 100 million nerve cells. If you get a tight, tense feeling in your stomach about something, take heed–something isn't resonating for you. On the other hand, if you get a bubbly, effervescent sensation, you're on the right path.

How do you know if it's real?

In *Behaving as if the God in all Life Mattered,* Machaelle Small Wright talks about how she used muscle testing to connect with nature and plants in her garden. She asked all kinds of yes or no questions to determine where to plant each seed, the direction of the rows, etc. She ended up growing 36-pound cabbages! Her advice is to always assume your intuition is right and act on it accordingly, and by doing so, you'll refine your ability to know if it WAS intuition or if it was your own mind telling you something. I often override my intuition, and then later, I understand exactly why my gut was telling me something different when things don't turn out well. For example, I'll get the nudge to drive a different way home, ignore it, and then get slowed down by an accident or construction.

I use intuition in determining my ad spend for new releases, often using a pendulum to get precise amounts. When I was releasing the book *Alpha Knight*, I heard to spend $500 per day on Facebook ads. I did, but the book languished. I was in Kindle Unlimited at the time, so watching my book rank on Amazon was important, and my goal was to keep it in the top 100. It took a lot more than $500/day to get it there and keep it there. I should have listened to my knowing, but my ego got in the way. I didn't want to see my book baby flop. I wanted it to be in the top 100—it meant something to me as an author. That I was good enough. Or successful enough. That my books were still relevant. So I pushed the ad spend.

If you're in Kindle Unlimited and have used the ad strategy I was using, you know that it's a gamble. You don't get immediate feedback on your return on investment because you get paid by page reads. The Amazon rank will

169

show you the quantity of downloads of the book, but you have to wait for everyone to read the book before you make your money.

Sadly, my *Alpha Knight* push was a total flop. Those page reads didn't come in. By the time I subtracted my ad spend from the income, I'd made a whopping eight thousand dollars.

Yes, I still made some money. I probably should've been celebrating. But I'd spent something ridiculous like eighteen thousand dollars to get there. I kept pushing and pushing ad spend on that book, determined to make it go, even though my gut had told me to back off.

Was it a failure? I certainly felt like it was at the time, but in retrospect and from an energetic perspective, no.

There are no failures.

I learned to trust my gut. I may not have profited much, but I reached a lot of people with those eighteen thousand dollars worth of ads. If you've heard of the law of seven, then you know that marketers believe people need to see your name or brand or product seven times before they buy. So I got one of my seven hits in for all the thousands of people who saw those ads and didn't buy.

Sometimes, we don't know the reason our gut guided us in a particular way. Yes, it could be that you're learning the lesson, like me, not to push against your knowing. But sometimes, we don't ever know the reason why. If you hear go left, you may not realize that your gut is preventing you from being in an accident because you have a safe drive. Sometimes, we figure it out (and make 20K like Megan Linski), and sometimes, we don't. Part of trusting your gut is exercising the believing-in-yourself muscle. The more you trust your gut, the more your trust, the more your intuitive muscle works. When you practice on the small nudges, you'll have the confidence to act on the big nudges (like putting all your books up for free).

Any time you're stuck and you're not sure what to do, ask the Universe to show you. Tell it to make the answer obvious, so you're not guessing hard or trying to interpret. While you're at it, tell it you'd love for the Universe to show you ease with the situation. Make it fun. Even lucrative (if appropriate to the situation). Ask it to create something greater for you.

Remember, as we discussed in Step 2, you don't need to worry about the "how"—just trust.

Home Play: Intuition Invitations

- **Every day this week, use your gut to choose your clothing for the day.** I like to close my eyes to clear my visual field, then set my intent to see the perfect thing to wear, then open my eyes and scan the closet with that intention. I'm often drawn straight to a certain top or color.
- **Use your intuition to pick the best excerpts / teasers for your next release.**

It's the same principle as the previous exercise. Open your manuscript on your computer (or hold the book in your hands if you have a physical copy) and set your intent to pick the best teasers or excerpts to share on social media or with book bloggers. Then drag the scroll bar down and stop when you get the hit to stop. Read on that page to find what is there that's perfect. If there's really nothing (which sometimes happens to me, but not often), don't get upset that it seemingly failed, just restart the exercise.

- **Use your intuition to determine ad spend on a campaign**

Don't try this if you're feeling nervous about it—only if it's fun. Use a pendulum or muscle testing to figure out how much to spend on an ad campaign. To use the pendulum, assign different angles of the pendulum different amounts. For example, the forty-five degree angle is ten dollars a day or less, ninety degrees is ten to twenty dollars, 135 degrees is twenty to thirty dollars. Once you get that answer, you could narrow it down further. Or write the ranges down on small pieces of paper, fold them, and mix them up. Lay them out on a table in a row and ask the pendulum to point to the one that will create the most profit for your book. When I am nervous that my own opinions are interfering with a clear answer from the pendulum, the scrap of paper method works better because I don't know what's on each of them.

To muscle test, ask the question, "is it less than $10/day? (test yes or no), then go on, depending on the answer you get. For example, if you got yes, then ask next, "Is it less than $5/day?"

- **Use your intuition to plan your writing schedule for the next twelve months (or further out, depending on how far you plan).**

Freewrite on the following questions:

- What projects are best for me to pursue next year with my writing career?
- Which series?
- Which book?
- Which one do I write first?
- When is the best time to release ___ book(s)?
- Which book or project will make me the most money?
- Which book or project creates more for my author career?

If you like, you can take your answers and further refine them into a plan by muscle testing for the exact order of books and release weeks. Then pay attention as you are working through your plan. The energy might shift, and suddenly you have the feeling something needs to move up (or down) on the list. Pivot using your new knowing.

- **Use your intuition for your current work in progress.**

freewrite to the following questions:

- What do I write next?
- What are the key elements to this book?
- What am I doing well?
- What needs more development?

Even if you just take five minutes to journal each morning for what you write next, it could change your entire relationship with writing. I know my word count skyrockets when I know what I'm going to write vs. when I sit down and try to figure it out in front of my computer screen.

Step 5: Live it Now

Chapter 12

Receiving

I
f manifestation is as simple as *ask, believe, receive,* then the next two steps would be the *receiving* part. You made your request or ask in Step 2, "Feed the Fire," when you set your intention. You worked on believing and releasing resistance to receiving with Step 1, "Clear the Deck" and all along the way through your written contemplations. Now it's important to open up to receive, and that involves becoming a vibrational match with what you're calling to you (Step 5, "Live it Now") and giving it space to appear (Step 6, "Let it Be"). There are many who believe that receiving is the most difficult part of manifestation. Intention setting is the fun part. The dreaming part. The feel-good place. But then we can block our manifestations from showing up in a variety of ways. Resistance can show up in limiting beliefs. Impatience. Operating from the past instead of the future you want to create.

In this step, you're going to start playing the part of the millionaire author. Becoming it now. When you wrap yourself in the energy of what you're calling to you, you actually already have it. You already feel abundant. Blessed. Grateful. You don't really want or need the thing you asked for. You're not in a state of lack.

One of the tricks to bringing in abundance is being willing to actually receive it. You think you're ready. You think you're willing, but if you don't actually believe you deserve it or that it will actually come, you block it from entering your life.

Several years in a row, I applied to be a signing author for the Shameless Conference but wasn't accepted (or so I believed). One year, Lee Savino called me up to say, "I got invited to Shameless!"

Oh. My shoulders sagged. "I didn't hear anything."

"I'm sure you're invited," she said, believing they wouldn't invite her without also inviting me. "Check your spam."

Sure enough, the invite was in my spam. My belief that I wouldn't be invited had blocked me from receiving it. How many years had I been invited but hadn't even received the invitation? Maybe that was my first year, maybe I'd been invited every year and just never knew it! For my ego's sake, I love to believe it was the latter.

Where are you blocking abundance, invitations, accolades, or even good reviews from coming with your doubt?

Sometimes we ask the Universe for something, and we're unprepared at how quickly it comes. So unprepared that we turn away opportunities.

Last year, I was playing with lucid dreaming. Dreams show us the direction our energy is headed, so I figure, if I can go lucid in a dream to imagine what I'm trying to create, then I'll program my energy for what I'm calling into being.

The first night, I just played with flying (because isn't that what everyone does when lucid dreaming?). The second night, I decided to pick something I wanted to manifest in my life. Since I had started writing this book, I decided to try to lucid dream myself as a speaker at author conferences, presenting this material.

Literally, the very next day, I received an email from an author asking if I'd give a presentation to a mastermind group she was part of.

Forgetting that this was the very thing I'd asked for the night before, I tried to deflect it back into the realm of what I already knew how to do–my present energy–and asked if they were looking for some coaching. Then, after I sent off the email, I remembered the lucid dream. *Gasp!* I shot off another email asking if she meant something more like a presentation.

She wrote back, "We'd like you to give a presentation, *like the sort of thing you'd give at an author conference."*

Whoa. I couldn't believe it! Lucid dreaming really worked for instant manifestation! But I was also a little terrified to receive what I'd asked for. Self-doubt about my ability to give such a presentation crept in. I still had the instinct to try to deflect it back to the more familiar territory of coaching.

But I know better than to refuse gifts from the Universe when they are offered. Especially when it's something I've asked for.

Remember–the Universe can't help you if you're not willing to receive.

Happily, that presentation for a small mastermind group has turned into two major author conferences this year. The Universe heard my request and promptly delivered. When I was willing to receive, it delivered more.

Really pay attention to the subtle ways you refuse or deflect the gifts that are offered to you. There can be a multitude of reasons–you feel unworthy of them, your self-image doesn't support having them, you have a habit of deferring praise or abundance to others.

When you find a penny, do you pick it up and thank the Universe for the abundance it sent you? When someone tells you *thank you*, do you respond with *you're welcome*? If someone "pays" you a compliment, can you receive it with gratitude, aka *thank you,* or do you immediately minimize (it was nothing, it was so easy), pass off (it wasn't me, it was the team), let it fall on the floor (blush and say nothing or laugh)? Receiving energy may sound like a small thing–tiny, really–but what you do with the energy tells the Universe you'll have more, *thanks*. That you're willing to receive. Don't refuse the gifts that are sent your way. Think about it. If someone says *thank you*, and you can't acknowledge and receive that energetic gift with a *you're welcome*, can you receive more (an invite to speak, a Bookbub, free promotion from the app you use)? If you can't receive the energetic gift of a compliment, can you receive physical energy, page turns, reviews, referrals, money? If you can't receive energy, and drop it on the floor, the Universe will give the energy to someone else who can. Receive with gratitude, and the gifts will multiply!

Observer Effect in Quantum Theory

Scientists have proven that by the very act of watching, the observer affects the observed reality. [1] I'd heard this bandied about with relation to manifestation for many years, but since I'm not a science-oriented person, the significance didn't really sink in until recently. I understood this was some of the science behind "our thoughts create our reality," which is cool, but I was already a subscriber to that theory. What I realized, though, is how important it is to keep this in mind when you're making your request to the Universe or asking for the thing to show up.

If the observer can shape atoms into what they're observing, you can see how important it would be to keep your focus on what you want versus what you don't want. If you look in the mirror and see someone who needs to lose weight, guess what? That's what you'll keep getting.

If you want your body to change, you have to practice observing wonderful things about your body. How strong you are. How fast your metabolism can be. How quickly you build muscle. Even if these things aren't showing up yet, find something you can observe or believe that will create what you'd like to see in the mirror. Clear your limiting beliefs around your body and practice becoming the observer who sees all the wonderful things about your body. When I find this magical mode, I will suddenly drop five pounds in a week, tighten up and look amazing. It's because I found something amazing about my body to appreciate, and then my body delivered more of that.

This is the explanation for the placebo effect–something I personally think ought to be studied and investigated as much as new medicine and treatments. When people believe they've taken the pill that will fix them or had the surgery to repair a joint, at least one-third, and sometimes up to sixty percent of them will experience actual healing. This is the power of belief.

How does this apply to books? Let's say you set an intention, asking the Universe to get your book to the top 100 on Amazon. Then you act as the observer, and sit back and look for evidence that it's happening. When you look for it, the molecules will transform and change to make it so! You watch the rank climb on a release day. Each change in your rank proves you're getting closer and closer. When it stops dropping and turns the other way, stop looking at that measurement and find another one that feels good.

Break success into tiny bites and celebrate every single win. When you are a six-figure author, a six-figure day is $274. I'll bet you've already had one! So, celebrate it. Celebrate every single one of them as six-figure days. Then you celebrate a six-figure week: $1923. Then you celebrate your six-figure months: $8333.

Celebration signals to the Universe that you'll have more of it. It brings your attention to what you want, not what you don't want, so the observer effect kicks into gear. We'll talk more about this in Step 7: Honor Yourself.

On my way to making a million dollars in one year, I broke the goal into tiny bites. I picked up my calculator and figured out what a million dollar day would be ($2739), so every time I hit that amount in a single day, I'd celebrate it as a million dollar day. Then I figured out what a millionaire month would be ($83,333), so when I hit that, I celebrated it as a millionaire month. Finally, as I observed all of these incremental wins, they started to accumulate. They happened more often. Eventually, I had a million-dollar year.

Conversely, if you look for evidence that your books will never hit top 100, well... can you see why that would be a bad idea?

Meditation: Money Pull and Receiving

Often we've created abundance somewhere in the multiverse, but it hasn't shown up in this timeline or in the present. This meditation is wonderful for pulling money into the here and now.

1. Close your eyes and imagine your energy like a ball of light around you.
2. Extend it out to the furthest reaches of the Universe.
3. Make the demand that the amount of money you desire show up now. You could say, "I'll have the money now, please" or even, "I demand the money show up now." Notice how there's a power and potency to demanding versus the energy of begging for money.
4. Open up to receive the abundance, allowing it to flow into your energy field and stay. You might picture it like a snowstorm of hundred dollar bills that swirl around you from all sides and stick to you like glue.

5. Feel the gratitude that accompanies that abundance—how the vibrations are the same. Turn up that sensation of gratitude. Revel in it for as long as you like.
6. Thank the Universe (or whoever you want to thank) for the abundance that is on its way to you.

Case Study: Mia Brody - Becoming a Full-Time Author

Just over a year ago, Mia Brody was working two online businesses and writing short stories on the side for her own amusement.

"I enjoyed my other businesses to a degree, but I always felt this restless creative energy. I just challenged myself to write every day for a thousand days as a stress relief outlet."

She discovered author Hope Ford, who was making a full-time living writing short fiction. "I was already writing short stories for my own amusement, so I figured—why not get paid for it? I had business skills and love fiction writing, so let's marry the two."

Mia began writing "short read" romance featuring cowboys and mountain men. She made a vision board focused on her fiction-writing career with a list of goals. "I love planning, organizing, dreaming. In order to achieve anything, you have to first cast the vision. If you don't have a vision, it's like getting in your car and just driving around aimlessly. You know you want to go somewhere, you just don't know where."

Part of her vision included leaving her two online businesses to be a full-time fiction author. "I knew from my other online businesses, if you make one dollar online, you can make five dollars. So I knew if I could make one thousand a month from my books, I could make five thousand. It took me six months to make that thousand, but I did it."

Unfortunately, a neuromuscular disease Mia has had suddenly flared up in a dramatic way right around the time she was publishing her first books. Despite being bedridden, she persevered, keeping her online businesses running while she built her fiction career.

"My mom gave me a laptop, and I started writing on that. I just kept going at it. I didn't know what else to do. I came to a point when I was writing the tenth book, and I watched two authors give up on their careers. I was at an all-time high with pain levels. I was sobbing as I wrote that book. But I thought, *If you give up, what are you going to do?*" She realized she would keep writing. She would still write the stories for her own amusement. So she figured she might as well keep going. "After that, I always set up a preorder book, so I couldn't give up or quit."

Mia ended up publishing 32 short reads in the span of fifteen months, which enabled her to shut down her other businesses and write fiction full-time. She more than replaced her former income with her books.

"I've seen authors start talking about manifesting, and they make the mistake of assuming that everything is going to be smooth sailing. Then when life inevitably happens, they get discouraged and throw their mindset work out the window. I don't want that to happen to anyone!"

Mia says she's proof that you can face really big obstacles and still manifest exactly what you want.

"I believe you should hold the vision but be flexible with your methodology to get there. It takes patience and time."

— *Mia Brody*

Chapter 13

How to Live it Now

Make a Kick-Ass Folder

My co-author and fellow abundance coach Lee Savino once gave me an assignment: Create what she dubbed a "Kick-Ass" folder. I made a virtual one in my email inbox. In it, I file away the nice emails readers send me and screenshots of reviews that make me feel good. Any accolades that prove I'm a "kick-ass" author. After about a month of using the folder, I received a huge boost in confidence. I'd previously been disheartened by a few bad reviews, yet there were so many nice emails to file! So many great reviews! When I compared those to the few negative reviews I received, they greatly outweighed them. Simply by making it a task to file away the good, it brought my attention to the positive. I guess I'd discounted all those lovely comments before because I'd trained my mind to look for criticisms. I'd been focusing on the things that made me feel bad about myself as a writer. What a great way to sink your own ship!

Please, if you take one thing from this book, let it be

making and utilizing your "Kick-Ass" folder. The act of creating it and filing things in it will instruct the Universe to send you more awesome responses to your work.

Expect Miracles

When I was a kid my dad used to subject us to self-help audiobooks on long road trips. He also made us practice meditating. Of course, that made me rebel and resist, and it took me a while to find my way back again.

Still, many of the nuggets I heard in his car have stuck in my head for all these years. One of them was a Tony Robbins anecdote about how race car drivers can't look at the wall because if they do, they'll crash right into it. They can only look ahead on the racetrack—they have to focus on where they want to go, and ONLY on where they want to go.

It's the same with tight-rope walkers. They never look down—they keep their gaze straight ahead on the place they're headed.

I remember putting this into practice stream-hopping in Alaska. If I looked at the next rock I wanted to step on, I'd safely land on it. But when I didn't choose a rock—when I panicked and thought *oh God, I'm going to land in the water*—that's when my foot would plop into the water. Was there a right way to get across the stream? Right rocks to step on? Nope. Any of those rocks would've worked. The point was just to keep stepping on rocks. There are no mistakes on our path. It's always leading us to our targets. Unless you focus on what you don't want like landing in the stream.

It's the same way for attracting success and abundance in our author careers. If you focus on where you want to go, you'll end up there. Focus on the negative, you'll get more of that. I'll bet you've seen this in action with relationships. The second something about your partner or child starts eating at you, it seems like they do more of it and more of it until it drives you bonkers. It's hard to flip a script with people you live with. I can easily go into crabbiness about my kids not doing their chores and being ungrateful for the dinners I make. But if I change the story into what I want– grateful, helpful, loving kids–(if I expect miracles!), they suddenly, miraculously, show up that way. Just this week my surly teenager started repeatedly signing (she's taking ASL) "Guess who loves you? Me!" and when I was helping her study for a test, said, "thank you for spending so much time with me, Mom." This is a kid who was all stomps and complaints just a few weeks ago.

In "The Luck Factor," Richard Wiseman reported the findings of a ten-year scientific study on luck[1] that proved people who believe they are lucky *are actually luckier* because they look for and see opportunities that people who think life is out to get them don't. He said, "Lucky people generate their own good fortune via four basic principles. They are skilled at creating and noticing chance opportunities, make lucky decisions by listening to their intuition, create self-fulfilling prophecies via positive expectations, and adopt a resilient attitude that transforms bad luck into good."

This is why it's important to be vigilant with your thoughts and energy around money. "I can't afford that" and "I'll never get there" won't create success and possibility. In the writing world, it might be "Bookbub hates me" or "I'll never be as successful as so-and-so" or even "I really need to up my game." Flipping these to something positive your mind will believe and accept are energetic game changers.

"Every time I submit to Bookbub, I get closer to being selected" or "Bookbub loves my books, and as soon as the timing works out, they'll pick me." You could futurecast it– "I'm so grateful I get picked for a Bookbub every freaking time I submit! Remember how I used to think they hated me? Ha! Now they ADORE me!"

We get what we look for and expect. Whether you believe the Universe magically delivers it or whether you believe it's the power of your subconscious taking the right steps once your belief has been programmed–either way–it's true.

So EXPECT MIRACLES. Every day. Expect them in every facet of your life.

That pain in your lower back? Decide that it's going to work itself out, and you don't need to worry about it anymore.

Getting a Netflix deal for your book? It's going to happen. Expect it. Picture it. Pick your ideal cast. Celebrate it like it's real. Imagine what shoes you'll wear to the celebration party. Make a vision board of it, with the character names and who's playing them.

Expect the miracles and celebrate when they show up for you. I knew they were coming to you all along.

Frame Things As If You Trust They Will Happen

"We're magic together."

For years, Lee and I used to intend the Bad Boy Alpha series earned millions. "This is our Million Dollar series," Lee would say playfully. The series was successful at the time, but nowhere close to earning millions. But we remained excited and happy. We kept publishing books.

Between August 2019 and February 2021, we took a break from publishing Bad Boy Alpha books and worked on other projects. Amazingly, the series kept making money. We started translating the Bad Boy Alpha books into different languages, and those translations sold really well.

At the end of 2020, I checked my dashboard and realized the Bad Boy Alpha series had earned over a million dollars in its lifetime. Without hard work, with great ease, the books crossed over that earning threshold. It became the Million Dollar series we pretended and projected it was!

Trying is Different than Trusting

For several years, I waffled over the decision to take my books wide or remain in Kindle Unlimited. I made great money in Kindle Unlimited but so did some of my close friends who were wide. So I decided to test it. I took one complete older series–my alien warrior romance series–and put it up wide.

This is what they tell you to do, right? Test things. Collect data. Make informed decisions? I'm not knocking that method. We should always have all the information available to us. I just believe that information is there with or without the data. It's there when you use your intuition. Every answer in the Universe is available to you at any time. I tell my high school student to pull the answers in on a test if she doesn't know them, and her "guesses" are stunningly accurate.

Anyway, I wasn't going with intuition on this one, I was using cold, hard data. I sat back and waited. I left it wide for a year. Collected the data. Compared how the series had done in Kindle Unlimited to how it had done wide. I found it did exactly the same. I made no more or less wide than I had in Kindle Unlimited.

And then I had a stunning realization. Energetically, I only *allowed* the numbers to be the same. I had a cautious, check-and-see energy, not the spaciousness it takes to invite something different. I suddenly knew that if I had gone "all-in" energetically with wide the way I had with Kindle Unlimited when I first found success there, I'm sure I could have created more.

As it turns out, a few years later I was forced out of Kindle Unlimited, and I doubled my income that year (you can read that story in the "Setbacks" section at the end of the book).

I hope you know this story is not to influence you to go wide or stay in Kindle Unlimited. It is about committing to success instead of dabbling. When you decide to make something work, to find success, you will. The Latin root of the word "decide" literally means "To cut off," as in you cut off all other possibilities. So when you decide to become a millionaire author, versus waiting to see how it goes, you send a very different, very powerful message to the Universe, and the Universe responds with everything you need to get there.

Feel Rich to Get Rich

Abundance is a state of mind, not the state of your bank account. You could have all the money in the world and still not feel rich. Conversely, you could feel abundant with less than the big figure you're shooting for. It has to do with the vibration of abundance.

No, this isn't another one of those posts to tell you to just be grateful for what you have because it's enough.

Reaching for more is the joy of being on this Earth in a physical body! Our bodies like to be treated. They want nice things. Our being wants to stretch and grow and achieve all the new things.

But the vibration of abundance brings more abundance. Gratitude and joy resonate at a higher frequency than lack and "why me?"

How can you use this to achieve your targets? Align with the things that make you feel good. Get the $5 coffee. Take the walk. Indulge and treat yourself in all the ways possible now. Don't deny yourself the jeans that fit your body perfectly or the expensive skin care product. And then really enjoy the splurge. Feel the abundance of it.

Send the message to the Universe that you think you're worth it and you love feeling abundant, and it will respond with more of the fabulous!!

Several years ago, I gave up gluten and sugar and took on coffee as a replacement "treat". To me, a trip to Starbucks was a reward. A comfort. A pick-me-up. I became a Starbucks rewards member, utilizing their star rewards to get even more coffee. That year, Starbucks initiated a game in which you could win "Starbucks for Life."

Oh boy, did the idea of that turn me on! It sounded so decadent. So rich. If I won that, I would feel so incredibly abundant. I played daily, winning a few things like a bag of coffee beans, a mug, a free drink. I gave it some thought– what would it be like to win? I did a little research and figured out that the winner would receive one free drink from Starbucks every day for the rest of his or her life.

So... one drink a day. I could actually afford that. And that's all it would take for me to feel incredibly abundant. All I had to do was stop denying myself that grande decaf cappuccino every day if I wanted one.

Why do it? If it made me feel like a millionaire, it was worth it! I'm worth it. Now, if I want one, I joyfully get it.

What makes you feel abundant? It might be something as small as a cup of coffee. Would having fresh flowers on your table or desk change your reality? I recently subscribed to a flower delivery subscription from ReVased where I get a bouquet delivered once a month. For each bouquet delivered, they also donate one to a nursing home, so I feel like I'm spreading the joy at the same time I'm treating myself. Giving and receiving—doubling my abundance.

Another one for me is buying organic blueberries. Yes, they sometimes cost twice as much as the non-organic. But berries absorb the highest amounts of pesticide of all fruit, and I also love them, so, for me, this is a great place to splurge.

Where are the places you deny yourself? What do you desire that evokes the feeling of abundance in you?

Home Play: Upgrades

Take $10-20 and go buy some small items that will make your life instantly better. Here are some ideas of what to buy:

- New pens: there's nothing worse than grabbing a pen to jot down a grocery list, only to have the ink sputter and die in the middle of the word "lettuce". It's the worst! You're a millionaire author, you deserve nice pens!
- Music: Would a subscription to Spotify, Apple eMusic or Amazon Music make you feel so wealthy? Then go for it. Treat yourself! Feel like a millionaire each time you enjoy the app!
- A nice pillow: You can never have too many cute pillows!
- Treat yourself to coffee, lunch, or a small dessert. Or buy a nicer brand of coffee or tea and a beautiful mug—these are other writer essentials.

- A new toothbrush or razor: You probably have a new one in a drawer under your bathroom sink. You just were holding off using it.
- Sexy panties or cozy socks. Whatever makes your body light up!

Ideally, you'd let yourself get rid of the old, grungy or useless items first. This can be surprisingly difficult. One of the reasons we hold onto old stuff is because we're telling ourselves: "I can't afford it. I'd better stick with the old because if I let it go now, I might need it later, and I might not have any money in the future to buy what I need. Plus, I don't want to waste money on myself. I don't deserve nice things."

I have a wealthy friend who when she got divorced kept all of the furniture she had from the marriage. She's bought and sold three houses, each time moving the old furniture in and each time not enjoying the house or feeling like it was a good fit once she was there. I've asked her, "What would it feel like if you had new furniture," and until recently, her answer was, "I don't want to give this furniture away or sell it for nothing—it was so expensive and is such great quality". In her most recent home purchase, she bought a new sofa, and for the first time in ten years, she told me, "I really feel comfortable sitting in my den. I like this house".

When you allow yourself to upgrade your life, the underlying message is "I am worth nice things. I trust I will have the money to buy what I need in the future." You're living "I am my abundance."

I'm not encouraging you to go on a spending bender and create financial ruin. What I'm saying is that we often deny ourselves small things that create huge energetic shifts. Do you write in a closet or a space that you hate because you're not worth claiming the space you really want to write in? Do you write in an environment that is uninspiring because you don't want to get in anyone's way or change what anyone else is doing or don't feel you can paint it or spruce it up? Does the price difference between organic blueberries and non-organic blueberries financially change your life, or does making that one choice to splurge make you feel like a million bucks each time you eat the blueberries? What I am encouraging you to do is to notice the things that you perceive as just beyond what you feel is possible and bring one of them into your life. See how it feels. When you see the thing you choose, do you light up? Do you feel your joy? Worth? Notice how you feel. If that worked, what's your next reach?

As an author, there are ways to invest in your business to move forward. When it comes time to get a new website, set up a newsletter, subscribe to Bookfunnel or Book Report, invest in Facebook ads or translations, do you allow yourself to act like the millionaire author you are? Or do you shrink and tell yourself you can't afford it?

I remember when I was using the free version of Mailchimp, and my list was growing. I was at a choice point. Do I take the leap to a paid version? I started researching paid options. I took the leap to what I felt was a stretch but worth it, and before long, I was at the next stretch. I trusted my gut, and before long, my list outgrew that leap too.

You don't have to spend money needlessly, but if your gut is telling you to increase your marketing budget, don't let your small self image stand in your way!

What Would a Millionaire Author Do?

I try to ask myself this question when I approach problems. My tendency is to think small. To make myself small. To approach situations like I'm small.

This idea of recasting your self-image is the old "fake it until you make it" strategy. Act as if you already have the life you're envisioning for yourself. When you do so, you make different decisions—decisions that value you and send the message to the world that you are a badass.

Often when I examine successful authors, I realize they're not so much better than I am in terms of the quality of the writing. Sometimes they are, and that's totally inspiring. But often, what I notice is that they are the ones who take their career and their books seriously. They're not projecting "I hope you like this book" with their energy. They're projecting "this is an awesome book, and I know it. And because I know it, I invested my money and my time to give the very best for it" energy. Whether that's a professional cover, a big launch, ad spend, or just a willingness to be seen, their belief in themselves and their books comes across energetically. Readers will assume you're an amazing author if you do.

Pretend you are a multi-million dollar author. You're a movie-optioned big-shot author. You're the author who, at book signings, has readers RUNNING to your table and standing in a long line to meet. You're that author. Now look at the problem/situation you're facing. Would you approach it differently?

Chances are, you'd make a different choice if you view the options from the perception of a million-dollar author. Lean in to that. Is the choice for the "lesser" option about fear of some kind of failure? Sometimes, when I'm facing a choice and feel afraid to pull the trigger, I lean in and leap, knowing that I'm at an edge and believing I'm worth the risk. Sometimes, those risks have paid off, and sometimes they haven't paid off in a way that I can quantify. Either way, I've expanded. I experienced something new that I learned from. I've exercised my bigshot attitude and muscle.

The more you can play in that energy of bigshot, the more you will entrain to it. You'll resonate with it, and the things in your life that match it will start to show up. You won't believe other authors are better than you. You won't believe your current work in progress sucks. You won't panic when the new release doesn't launch as big as you expected, because Millionaire Authors know one book doesn't make or break their careers.

Think of it like Method Acting. You're going to embody the part of *Millionaire Author* and fully live in it—full time. Fun, right?

Find other successful authors you look up to and notice what they do. Follow them on social media, subscribe to their newsletters, read their books and take their courses. Our brains naturally change our behaviors to fit into the crowd, so surround yourself with successful people—it works even if they don't know who you are. Lee calls these her author models. They are typically uber-successful indie authors sitting at the top of the charts in paranormal and contemporary romance.

This practice is not about mimicking the other author or forcing yourself into someone else's mold. It's about trying out different energy. Sometimes we want to shift, but we don't know how. We're willing to stretch or reach, but we don't even know how to do it. I wanted to live like a billionaire author and look like one. But I'd been buying the same kind of clothes I always had. I didn't know how to dress differently. I didn't know how to choose something different. I had these perceptions of my body type, shape, finances, etc. I went shopping with my friend, Melody Edmondson, author of Your Fashion Guide Based on Body Shape & THE SPACE OF THE WAIST®. Melody is an expert on dressing people based on their body shape. She helped me see myself differently, choose different shapes and colors, mix and match in a different way. To never miss an opportunity to look great. To try on and wear different clothes. And that's what author models can do. Help you perceive with expansion.

Notice the kinds of authors in your circle. Are they primarily positive? Do they function from an abundance mindset, or would they be open to playing with this mentality with you?

Dwell in gratitude for the successful authors around you. Whenever there's drama in the author community, remind yourself of the positive people in your circle and choose to spend more time appreciating and loving them.

Millionaire Author Day

Remember in Step 2 when you wrote about what your ideal day as a millionaire author would look like? You can have it now!

Celebrate your Millionaire Author status (that's on its way to you now) by taking a "Millionaire Day." A millionaire day includes all the things you'd do as a millionaire. It might be to wake up at a leisurely hour, drink a cup of espresso or your favorite tea, write by the ocean or in a fun cafe, meet a friend for lunch, go to a yoga class and maybe get a facial or massage. In the evening, go to your favorite restaurant or see a movie you've been wanting to see.

Just like starting to track and celebrate your small wins every time you have a day that equals out to what a six-figure or seven-figure author averages in a day, you're going to start to indulge yourself like you're already there—one day at a time.

It's okay if you don't have a lot of money to spend yet. You could drive to the closest resort in town, sit on their fancy patio and order a glass of wine. While you're there, work on any beliefs you might have that you don't belong there, that you don't fit in, that you can't have that life. You're having it! You're choosing it right now! You don't have to break the bank to get the feeling of being a million-aire. It's creating the time and space for an indulgence of the senses and surrounding yourself with wealth.

I had never stayed at a Four Seasons before Skye Warren offered the first Romance Author Mastermind conference there. I was so grateful to her for choosing that site because it was a chance for me to feel like a millionaire author. I was greeted at reception with a glass of cham-pagne, then served a second free glass when my room wasn't immediately ready. I was surrounded by luxury. There were famous people in the hotel bar! *Drake* was there, and a U.S. Senator. (Okay, *I* didn't see any of these famous people, but I heard they were there.) Also, the toilet paper in the bathroom by the lounge was black. Black! *Fancée*, as my teenager would say (that's fancy pronounced with a French accent). Just being in that environment changed my world, and it was just for a weekend!

Window Shopping for your Future Life

Just like having a glass of wine at a fancy resort can be nour-ishing, so can trying on designer clothes, test-driving new luxury cars, or walking through multi-million dollar homes for sale. You're taste-testing. Immersing yourself in the energy of the future you're creating right now in the present moment.

You want to give yourself the physical sensations, treat your body to the deliciousness that will be yours to get you excited about, and feel deserving of having it. We want you to get used to luxury, so the Universe starts showing up with it effortlessly. Splurge on valet parking and get used to being treated like royalty.

If you have a place to shop for designer clothing nearby, go and try on a ten thousand dollar Gucci or Prada dress. Or try Rent the Runway where you can rent designer outfits for a special occasion or just to feel like a million bucks!

What's your dream car? Why don't you go and test drive a few now? Find out how it feels to sit behind the wheel? Receive the luxury and joy of it now, so you can already have the energy of it.

Upgrades You Can Make Today

One of the concepts I utilize the most from Denise Duffield-Thomas' book *Get Rich, Lucky Bitch,* is the idea of making incremental upgrades now to invite abundance. Figure out if there's an upgrade you could make to your life right now that would make you feel luxurious, wealthy, supported or nurtured.

Can't afford the sheets? Get the pillowcase. Purchase something tangible that makes you feel rich every time you use or see it. How about fresh flowers on the table? (Hint: Costco and Trader Joe's have gorgeous flowers for cheap.) Let the thing you chose be your ***millionaire token***–a reminder that you see or experience every day that reminds you of the life you're going to have. Maybe you buy a special keychain that represents success (I've seen some that say "rich bitch" or are in the shape of money bags). Pick anything that reminds you or feels luxurious.

Here are some suggestions:

- Hire a housecleaner once or twice a month (this is life-changing!).
- Hire a personal assistant to handle your newsletters (or even just offload something small for $5 on Fiverr!).
- Try a food delivery box that delivers meal kits or ready-made meals.
- In the writing cave? Order Door Dash or Grub Hub to deliver your coffee or lunch to you, so you can stay in the zone. Or get an Instacart delivery of your groceries or just snacks!
- Have breakfast in bed! (I used to love bringing my coffee back to bed to stay under the covers writing for a couple hours.)
- Take a bubble bath with candles and a face mask.
- Go to a beauty school where they need people to try out spa treatments for a low-cost day spa experience. It's the same products they use in a spa, and the aesthetician is a student, but they're very careful and attentive since they're still learning (and they're supervised).

Own the Energy of Luxury

One time, my co-author Lee and her friend visited from Virginia to try out a very expensive posh spa outside Tucson called Miraval. The way the fees work at Miraval, two people can share the cost of the $1200/night room, but there's no break for a third person. In other words, I would have to pay a full $1200/night to go and stay with them. I opted, instead, to get a day pass and bunk in their room one night before going back to my own house. Unfortunately, that solution gave me a sneaky, undercover, *I don't belong here* feeling.

Of course, the Universe delivers what you're vibing.

When we arrived, despite the instructions they gave me on the intercom at the gate to come to the front circle for valet parking, I guess I was still feeling less-than, so I chose to park my own vehicle.

A spa employee–the valet driver, perhaps, came out to the parking lot where I'd parked. Instead of welcoming me and asking if he could take my bags, he chided me for not coming to valet parking! Not only that, he then *asked me to straighten my car out within the lines* because I hadn't parked it well enough!

I had to get back in my car and straighten it out to please him! It was utterly absurd, but that was the experience I attracted by bringing my less-than energy to Miraval.

Wow. Totally not the rich-person luxury queen bee experience I was hoping for.

As we walked in, Lee looked around at the beauty and opulence–the waterfalls and crystal sculptures. "Wow, what if this was your life?" she asked, obviously in the same I-don't-belong-here energy as I was.

But then she was smart enough to recognize it. "Wait a minute," she corrected. "This *is* my life!"

When you make your incremental upgrade or test drive the new Porsche or whatever it is, remember my story. Don't be in the middle of something that's supposed to be luxurious and push it away by feeling like you don't deserve it. Don't feel like you're sneaking in, borrowing it from the real rich people.

Really open up to receive the experience. Affirm that you deserve this and better. That you'll have this and better. Affirm that you belong there, you deserve nice things, nice experiences, and to be treated like royalty. Then bookmark the feeling. Name it or assign a symbol to it, so you can feel and embody it again, so you can call on the energy every time you think about your future life.

When I was looking for my new house, I wanted vaulted ceilings because that was my symbol for rising up. For having my own space. Every time I pictured my perfect house, I would feel this lifting up, looking out higher windows with a loftier perspective. This is how I called the perfect house to me.

Freewriting: Tap into Your Genius

freewrite answers to the following questions:

- How can I immerse myself in luxury today? (Is it getting 1000 thread count Egyptian cotton sheets for your bed? Is it buying a feather pillow?)
- What can I choose to be my Millionaire Author token or symbol, and what is the energy it embodies?
- What am I denying myself that if I would indulge would make me feel rich?
- Where could I have more possibilities and ease in my life?

Chapter 14

Embodying Your Future Self

Be Vigilant with your Words

As I mentioned before, the words you choose are important. Notice every time you say something like, "I wish I could afford that" or "Some day" and rephrase it to "I'm choosing that" even if for now, you're just choosing the energy of it until it actually shows up in the physical plane for you. Don't let lack or negativity creep into any of the words you choose about anything. As soon as they slip out of your mouth (as they inevitably will until you retrain your mind to observe what's right in your world instead of what's wrong), stop and rephrase it into something that will create your future rather than decay it.

Here are some examples of things writers might catch themselves saying:

- My new release sucked.

Reframe: More and more people find and love my book every day.

- No one is going to buy my book.

Reframe: The right people will find and love my book. I'm open to infinite possibilities for it.

- I can't figure out how to make Facebook ads work for me.
- **Reframe: I'm figuring it out.**
- Yeah, but I can't have the same success as so-and-so because…. (fill in the blank–they already have a huge following, they can afford a PR company, they have a whole team, they have money to spend on marketing, I can't write as fast as she does, I write longer/shorter/darker/lighter/standalones [insert excuse]). If you're having challenges with this, see Chapter Twenty on Jealousy / Competition.

Reframe: I'll have that, too!

- My books don't sell as well as hers.

Reframe: My books sell!

- I can't afford ___ [professional covers, ads, custom photography]

Reframe: I am choosing where to invest my money.

. . .

Policing your speech can get tiring and shouldn't become another way of making yourself wrong, so if you find you get down about how many negative things come out of your mouth about yourself and your books, just remind yourself that it's a habit. It takes a while to break a habit, but the more you practice, the easier it gets.

> The more you align your speech, thoughts, and energy to be congruent with your dreams, the quicker they can manifest!

Millionaire Author Playlist

Music has a wonderful way of building or enhancing a certain state. Melancholy music is great if you're writing an emo scene. Peppy music if you're trying to exercise. How about making a playlist that makes you feel like a million bucks? They don't have to be songs about money, but they could be. They should be songs that make you feel empowered, one of a kind, hopeful, expecting greatness.

I love songs like "It's a Perfect Day" from *Legally Blonde*, "A Million Dreams" and "This is Me" from *The Greatest Showman*, and "Don't Stop Me Now" by Queen. I made a playlist on Amazon Music that I can put on, and it puts me in the right energetic state to slay. Go make yours now. Update it often, and it will become another area where you bring attention to things that you make you feel good that will change your entire future.

Reimagine your Past

In *Becoming Supernatural*, Dr. Joe Dispenza said, "You can't create a new future holding onto the emotions of the past."

We can't change the past, right? Maybe not, but we can change the energy of the past. We can release the pain, or even... reimagine the past as something that provides us with the good-feeling emotions today.

Think about all the movies where the hero or heroine goes back in time, like *Back to the Future* or *17 Again,* and their retake of their past completely changes the future. When the character gets to the pivotal fork in the road moment, they make the same decision they made the first time around, they just feel differently about it.

You can do this energetically! You don't need the magic janitor, the time machine, or a movie crew. It's easier than you think to go back–all you need is your imagination.

I had a friend who became a single mother quite young, and she really wasn't up for it. She lacked patience with her son and felt like he was a burden, especially during his youngest years. He is an adult now, and she wanted to somehow heal their past and make amends for the energy she'd projected at him as a child, so she REIMAGINED all those past moments. On his first day of kindergarten, she was right there, holding his hand, nurturing him. During his soccer games, she was there cheering him on. She imagined picking him up, holding him, being there for him. She said the more she did this, the more their present relationship completely transformed. She didn't tell him what she was doing, but he somehow received her love and the way they were together softened into something new.

Recently, I had this vision of what my life would've

looked like if my parents had had a wonderful marriage instead of a fractured one. Our home would've been filled with love, sex-positivity, and exuberance. I would've carried that forward into my own marriage instead of living in the anxiety of things inevitably ending.

Huge hint—this exercise isn't to feel bad about what didn't happen, it's to actually rewrite the past, to transform the energy as if something great DID. To Re-envision.

Scientifically, the brain can't tell the difference between an imagined activity and a real one. And we know metaphysically there is no time, so the past is really the present is really the future. If you change the patterning of your past, simply by reenvisioning it the way you wish it could've been, and receive the energy of that, you're a totally different person. A potent, fulfilled, powerful person who knows they can create anything.

Try it—think of one less than positive thing that may have shaped you and rewrite it. For me, apart from my parents' divorce, what popped in my mind was my experience on my high school pompon team. I didn't realize it had shaped me, but I'm sure it did. Talk about mean girls! It was a horrible year for me.

So I just played with the scenario. What if it had been the best experience of high school? What if I'd been their star dancer instead of the outcast? The energy I received was wonderful. I felt confident, joyful, expansive. Happy.

So now I'm creating my future from that past instead of the old one. So much better, right?

But what if I can't pretend it's not true?

If you suffered a trauma you use to define yourself, you may resist this exercise. You feel like you can't pretend something that isn't true. It happened, it was real, and you need to deal with it.

Okay–so—what can your brain accept? Maybe simply a reframe of the events. This might be like looking for the silver lining of the event. For example, you were in a car accident that left you crippled. What if that was a gift? Maybe during your long recovery, you discovered a love for books and decided that you could be an author. What if that event was exactly what you needed to get you to where you are now?

Does coming from that energy, rather than one of tragedy or feeling like a victim, change your past, present, and your future?

When my tragically shy daughter was in kindergarten, she broke her leg and got to spin around in the cutest little wheelchair you've ever seen. She received an unbelievable amount of attention in that wheelchair, and the gift was that–for the first time–she started engaging with the adults who spoke to her. The Universe gifted her with a large heaping of positive attention, and it was enough to coax her out of her shell.

Home Play: Rewrite Your Story

Rewrite your story, casting yourself as the hero or heroine. How would things be different? Would the event be different, but just have a reframe? For example, you could take an incident when the mean girls of high school were saying crap and instead of shrinking, you'd know in that moment they were just small and insignificant bullies, and you were perfect just as you were?

Or would you actually change the story to make yourself Homecoming queen, the girl who got asked out by the high school soccer star or the Valedictorian who got a full ride to Stanford?

What would you change? How would that changed past affect your present? How does the energy feel now?

Whether you reframe that traumatic experience with you recast as the hero/heroine and the same facts, or you do a complete makeover, it will change the energy of today.

Meditation: Hot Tub Time Machine

In the Author Abundance monthly membership, I led a "Hot Tub Time Machine" meditation in which you travel to meet your future self–the one who has already achieved everything you seek to achieve.

1. Close your eyes and imagine you are entering the most luxurious hot tub. Maybe it's the kind with a waterfall. Maybe it's filled with salt water.
2. You step into the hot tub, and it transports you to another time or dimension. One in which you already are the successful, *New York Times* Bestselling Millionaire author, or whatever it is you're striving for.
3. Climb out of the hot tub and stand face to face with your alternate self. You may want to reach out and hold her hands, or look into her eyes.
4. Check in–what does she want you to know? What message does she have for you? What advice?

5. Synchronize your energy with hers.
6. Open up to receive any encouragement, love, or gratitude from her.
7. Thank her and return to the hot tub to transport you back to the current time-space reality.
8. Open your eyes and go out into your day with the gifts or information you received from your alternate self.

Freewriting: Tap into Your Genius

- Where do I want to be as an author in five years?
- Put yourself there—imagine it's already happened. What does my life look like?
- What am I doing differently? Better?
- Is it something I can already integrate today? How?
- What is one thing I could do immediately that would improve my lifestyle?
- What is one thing I could do immediately that would improve my career?
- What's the next step for me in my writing career?
- What blocks me from being the brilliant millionaire author that I am? Imagine that block, and recast it, reenvision it, rewrite it.

Step 6: Let it Be

"There will be an answer. Let it be." —The Beatles

Chapter 15

Do Less to Receive More

T his step can be the hardest, especially if you're a workaholic doer like me. We believe we have to keep our nose to the grindstone in order to achieve. But that doesn't always allow enough space for the magic and miracles to happen.

Control or holding on too tightly is an expression of lack.

When you try to control, are impatient, think you're the only one who can do things, you're repelling abundance from coming.

Letting go and trusting in the Universe opens your energy to receiving and puts you in a state of reception, so when there is a to-do, you know it, hear it, and have time to act on it. And you'll find those tasks are so easy to finish!

One of the ways I manage to produce more books (and income) but do less is co-writing. I'm not suggesting that you should run out and find a co-author, it's just one possibility that has worked for me.

When you co-write, you have someone to share not just

227

the writing tasks, but the marketing and administration, as well. Yes, you are sharing the profits, but I've found that the sales on co-written books are higher, probably due to the extended reach of two authors with two mailing lists, and two audiences.

Co-writing can take many shapes and forms. I work with each of my co-authors in different ways. With one, we volley back and forth, section by section until the book is complete. With another, we alternate taking the lead on books. One writes, the other follows and fluffs. In some cases, co-writing could be as easy as adding your name to a book someone wrote in your world and sharing the profits. I will say that there are certain personality types that are better suited to co-writing than others. Trust your gut. If you're considering co-writing with someone, pick someone whose books you love to read. Listen to the answers to the following questions:

Will working with this author create more?

What would my career look like in three years if I collaborate with this author?

You Don't Have to *Do*. You Just Have to Allow

Would you believe that sometimes all your career needs is a little space? If you're addicted to doing rather than being or allowing (I'm raising my hand), I highly recommend Denise Duffield-Thomas' book *Chillpreneur*. She has great advice on simplifying your tasks, batching, and delegating. I also recommend Tim Ferriss' *The Four-Hour Work Week* because he describes going from working twelve hour days to making the same amount working four hours a week.

If you're controlling your career or life too much, you

don't leave room for the quantum entanglements to work. You might miss being in the right place at the right time. You deflect a major opportunity because it didn't fit your plan for the year.

Katherine McIntosh, author of *Don't Diet, Be Happy*, explains it this way. You don't make a reservation at the restaurant and then call them back every twenty minutes to make sure they've got it. You trust that your reservation will be there for you when you get there.

The same goes for your requests to the Universe. You've made your request. You've envisioned your best life. You're loving your books, acknowledging yourself, feeling gratitude for all you've already achieved. Now just let it be.

Case Study: Maggie Dallen - Doing Less to Receive More

Sweet Young Adult and Historical Author Maggie Dallen has struggled with anxiety her entire life. In just first grade, she was so afflicted that she was sent to the doctor's office from school with a severe panic attack. "I've been searching my entire life how to be free of all this," she said.

In college, her dad bought her an Abraham-Hicks book to help with the anxiety. She theoretically understood the Law of Attraction, but every time she'd have a minor win, she'd try to take control. "I thought I was controlling it [her wins] with my thoughts."

She said the big lesson she finally learned is that she's not in control of anything. "I am choosing, but I'm not the one making it happen. I just choose what I want," she explained.

In 2017 she made $7,000 from her entire writing business for the year. She signed up for Denise Duffield-Thomas's Money Bootcamp. "I did the EFT and worked through blocks I hadn't known I had. Like magic, I went from $7,000 in a year to six figures the next." But Maggie's anxiety kicked in almost instantly. "I got really anxious about it–worrying about how to keep this happening. I instantly forgot that *I* didn't do it, that the Universe had."

Over the next few years, she started choking the life out of her business. "I had a death grip on it. I was a workaholic control freak, and the more I worked, the worse my sales did."

In March 2021, Maggie took her first vacation after two and half years of putting out 25 books a year. "It was the first time I relaxed in ages." During her vacation, she celebrated the fact that after all that work, she'd finally seen a significant increase in income. But then she received a call from her CPA informing her that since her income went up, she now owed more money in taxes. "That sent me off the deep end. I had the worst panic attack since I was a kid," she said. "All those years of working myself to the bone, and it felt like I just kept running into a brick wall."

She was reading Gabby Bernstein's book *Superattractor* at the time. "I started reading the chapter about being a workaholic and a control freak, and about how it's just a manifestation of fear."

She observed, "It makes sense that self-publishing calls to control freaks. We get to control every aspect." In some cases, Maggie said, we think we have the plan, but there might be another avenue or route to success that could be better.

> "I spent so much time running into a brick wall when really there was a perfectly nice doorway right to my left. I could've just opened the door and gone through."
>
> — *Maggie Dallen*

Realizing she never wanted to have another panic attack in her entire life and that she didn't want to be the kind of stressed-out mom she'd been, she knew she could either choose to live in fear and be a control freak or let it all go and trust things would work out and be okay.

"I feel so grateful for the anxiety issues because it led me to this moment," she said. She chose to surrender control. To "let it be."

"From that moment on, my husband would find me tapping constantly, to let it go. I just let things go that didn't feel good." She backed out of deadlines, timelines, and all commitments that didn't feel good to her. For a few months, she feared her business might collapse because of all the things she let go of.

"It was a lot of deprogramming. I was raised in a family where you work hard. I was bragging that I got up at 4 a.m to get this done, and feeling a sense of pride in my exhaustion, but really, who was I impressing?"

Of course, when you make space, things come into place naturally. Miracles can happen.

Maggie, who normally writes PG, mentioned to a friend that she had an idea for a steamier historical series. Her friend spoke with a publisher, who contacted Maggie and asked for that series. She also, very organically, started co-writing with a friend. She now has two other active pen names—one for the steamy historical and one for the co-written sweet. Both are far more lucrative than her original pen name.

Another synchronicity happened with screenwriting. "In November, I saw this ad for a screenwriting course, so I went and loved it." She particularly resonated with one of the speakers so when, a month later, she found out the woman was offering a small group mentorship, she jumped to get in.

Her mentor advised her to start adapting the book that lit her up, rather than the one her logical mind told her would do better. She did, and three weeks later, her mentor had shared it with a producer who loved it. Two weeks after that she'd signed a shopping agreement. "I got more validation in one month of writing screenplays than in twenty years writing books!" she said.

Her takeaway was, "Let go more, trust more, only do things you want to do."

This summer she continued to choose ease over work. Wanting to spend more quality time with her young son, she canceled her summer release plans. "My son is at the best age. He's five and just wants to play. I know he's not going to always want cuddle time like he does right now."

As it turned out, doing nothing suited her. "In June I made triple what I usually make," she reported. "I had some Tiktok success and a good release. It would look like luck from the outside, but for me, I know I allowed it to happen. I'm getting better at allowing it to happen and not feeling like I have to work so hard to make it happen."

Now, Maggie has made doing less a permanent practice. "I'm trying to find that balance because I truly love to work but it's all too easy to lose the fun and start trying to take control. I'll be having fun working, then suddenly I have that death grip again. I'm getting better about catching myself when I reach that point. When I get there, I make myself take a day off. I go do yoga, or take my son out to a movie, and I don't let myself work. Now I look forward to when I work hard because I know it means I get a day off."

She said, "It's been over a year since I've had that

moment, and it's been a freaking miracle. Sometimes I don't even recognize this new person I've become. I'm so glad I'm figuring it out when I am."

Chapter 16

Trust in Divine Timing

W hen manifestations haven't shown up yet, we have the tendency to wonder what we're doing wrong. You start looking for something you can control or do to fix it.

Sometimes there's timing involved for the quantum entanglements to work. Maybe you haven't written the book yet that will get optioned by Netflix. Maybe the idea for it will drop into your head while you give your career and books space. While you dwell in trust and openness to possibilities.

Take the pressure off achieving your goals by pretending it's already happened (as in Step 5). Trusting it's on its way to you.

After I married at age thirty, I wanted to start a family. I went off the pill and...nothing happened. So, being a doer, I starting doing. I read books on fertility. I tried every super-stition (I hung chopsticks in the corner, got rid of the metal framed bed, removed my belly button piercing). I took Chinese herbs and tried acupuncture. I held my knees to my chest after sex. After a year and a half, I finally got preg-

Renee Rose

nant. And then I miscarried. It was heartbreaking. I grieved, healed, and started the process of trying to get pregnant all over again. I had so much anxiety tied up in getting pregnant. I was already into law of attraction and manifesting outcomes back then. I knew I didn't want to be in resistance, so every morning I would thank the Universe in advance for the baby that was on its way to me.

It was a lot of efforting. A full time job for my energy and my psyche.

I went to see two different psychics who both told me the same thing: the baby is waiting for the right timing to come in. It makes sense. If you believe that we choose our parents and when and where we're born before we ever come in, then it stands to reason that the baby might have chosen a certain time to be born. That certain time did not track with the time I was hoping to conceive and give birth.

Eventually, three years after I started trying, I got pregnant and carried to term. Looking back now, from the perspective of a mother with two healthy teenagers, I just wish I could go back and give my thirty-year-old self a big hug. To tell her to relax and have faith–that it would happen.

But I was operating from lack. I didn't trust my gut, which told me I was meant to be a mother. I was too afraid the thing I wanted most in this world would never happen for me.

If only I'd known about this magical step: Let it be. To trust in divine timing. That we can't control everything. We're not supposed to do anything. And when our dreams haven't shown up yet, it doesn't mean we're doing something wrong, not doing enough or need to change. It just might need a little space. A tincture of time.

If I'd trusted that, I'd have the children I so desperately

wanted, AND I could've enjoyed those three years it took to have my first baby. Instead, they were a terribly tender, painful time for me.

Sometimes the best thing you can do for your career or your future is to get out of your own way. You sent your request out to the Universe, now give it time and space to gel. Open up to receive without trying to control the outcome.

Freewriting: Tap into Your Genius

Freewrite on the following prompts:

- What areas of my career and life am I trying to control that if I'd just let go would finally bloom?
- What decisions have I made about the things I need to do or the order they need to happen that may be limiting my possibilities?
- How have I decided success can happen for me? Are there other ways it might happen?
- What infinite possibilities are available for my books? My career?
- Where do I allow for the magic of the Universe in my life?
- Imagine that you have surrendered to the magic of the Universe. Feel into that. What does it feel like? Explore that place of freedom.

Chapter 17

Hit the Easy Button

Ask the Universe - Show Me the Ease / Fix It

I had a lot of anxiety around getting divorced, as you might imagine. I decided to DIY the divorce paperwork, not wanting things to get contentious or adversarial by lawyering up. On the day I went to file the paperwork I'd prepared, I was a bundle of nerves. This is another moment that, in retrospect, I wish I could go back and give myself a huge hug and whisper in my ear that it was all going to be painless. A piece of cake, even.

But I was wound up tight, feeling the significance and finality of the act, and certain disaster lurked in every corner. As I drove to the courthouse, I begged the Universe to *show me the ease*.

It's a tool I learned from Access Consciousness—to ask my body or the Universe to show me the ease. Depending on the situation, you can add on the tag, "and make it obvious or lucrative or fun."

In this case, I was just looking for ease. Problem number one with the courthouse was where to park. I wasn't sure if the downtown building had underground parking, whether it was open to the public, or what the scoop was.

As I approached the building, though, I spotted street parking, one of two spots, *right in front of the building*.

Okay, wow, I thought. The Universe has my back. *Whew*. I parked and got out, grabbing some quarters for the meter. When I got to it, I discovered it was still full. Whoever had parked here before left me with a full hour. Another kind gesture from the Universe.

I went through security and got inside the building where I asked for directions. I found the right floor, took a number, and had a seat. Less than a minute later, I was called to the window to deliver my paperwork. Let me tell you–I was nervous. My dad was an attorney, and I worked for him summers during college. I used to have to deliver documents to the courthouse for filing. I remembered that if you didn't have your paperwork just right, they had zero patience for you. Since I hadn't used an attorney and didn't know what I was doing, I was afraid this could go badly.

But again, I asked for ease, and that's what I got. The clerk couldn't have been more kind. She went over the paperwork, checking to make sure I'd done everything right and explaining the entire process to me. She also told me how lucky I was–that normally on Fridays, there were long lines at her window.

I felt truly blessed. I asked for help, and it had shown up.

When I came back for my court date, once again, the Universe conspired to give me helpful support. I was sitting in a hallway chair, and a (hot) dad from my son's elementary school walked by and spotted me. He came over, crouched down in front of me, and asked if I needed any help. He said he was an attorney, and his office was right around the corner if I did. It was terribly sweet and showed me that if I'm open to receiving it, there is assistance and support everywhere.

Universe fix it is another great tool to get out of your own way when things are going wrong. By assigning the problem to the Universe or to your energetic team, you stand back, surrender control, and allow good to happen when you're focused on the bad.

It gets you out of resistance and into flow with things. You know that because you turned your problem over to the Universe, it will be handled, and you no longer have to fixate, focus, work, do, harbor emotions about, or energetically block the solutions to this problem anymore.

When Lee Savino and I formed a new LLC to manage our co-written books, we opened a new KDP account, published our first book and...KDP shut down our account because they thought we had stolen the book (from ourselves!). It could have been upsetting. It certainly was a little frustrating. But the two of us knew enough about energetics to know that getting frustrated throws up blocks to getting things fixed. We asked the Universe to fix it for us. We also still called and emailed almost daily until it was resolved, but without having a huge negative charge on the issue. We trusted the Universe would sort things out for us, and it did. You may have also heard the phrase "Let go and let God." If this resonates more for you—use it!

Where could you request more ease? Are there places you're trying to control? Feeling like if you don't do it, it's not going to happen—and then what?! Fearing disaster? Ask the Universe to show you the ease or delegate the problem to the Universe to fix. Ask what infinite possibilities are available in that situation. By doing so, you invite them in to come and play with you. And when possibilities come to play—the magic happens!!

Stop Trying to Get it Right (there is no wrong!)

According to Gary Douglas and Dain Heer, founders of Access Consciousness®, the need to be right is one of the biggest distractors that keeps us from creating the life we want. I noticed this around the 2020 pandemic. People became so polarized when they chose their sides—maskers vs. anti-maskers. This is horrific vs. it's just another flu. Decisions were made about the right way to do things, and then judgment was heaped out when others didn't follow.

The need to be "right" keeps us distracted from following the energy, tapping into magic and receiving. As I learned to master all things in the author marketing world, I was always trying to get it right. I wanted to learn the method that worked and then prove again that it worked.

I would figure out one way to do Facebook ads, and it would work well, and then I'd get wrapped up in proving my method worked best. I wanted not just to get it right, but to *be* right. I would try that one way again and again, ignoring when it didn't work on a particular book. Or maybe ignoring the awareness that the strategy had stopped working in general. But my need to be right made me pour money down the drain trying to prove something to myself. A better strategy would have been to use my intuition as a guide. To ask each book how much to spend on it. Whether to push hard on ads or pull back.

This attachment to "right" and on the flip side, the aversion to being "wrong," is a great way to lose sight of your targets. When we're open, when we're flexible, when we don't have anything to prove, that's when the magic can happen. Thinking we know the one "right" way to do something is a fallacy that keeps us from pivoting when we need to pivot. Keeps us from hearing the whispers of inspiration, or following our gut instincts instead of conventional wisdom. Remember, you can always ask your books what they need!

Clinging to a certain point of view can limit you. It's like you're narrowing your focus on one piece of the landscape. If you zoom out, you see so much more of the picture.

Use the freewriting prompts below to discover where you're trying to get it right or afraid of getting it wrong. Can you leave both of these behind and go back to the simplicity of the third step to author abundance—*love your books*? That's the energy you want to be in. Nothing to prove. Nothing to fear. You don't have to have all the answers. They will show up at the exact time you require them.

Freewriting: Tap into Your Genius

Freewrite to the following prompts:

- Where am I trying to "get it right?" / What am I afraid of getting "wrong?"
- What am I trying to prove? Who am I trying to prove it to?
- Where have I been conditioned to do or be or believe something?
- What have I already tried and "failed" that I've decided I will never do again?
- What do I believe will never work for me?
- What limiting decisions have I made or conditions set like If I have _____ then _____.
- Where do I limit myself? What infinite possibilities are available in this situation?
- Think about something that's going on in your life right now that you'd like to turn over to the Universe. With love in your heart and that

situation in your consciousness, ask: what else is possible over and over again. Just allowing for possibilities to show up.

Step 7 - Honor Yourself

Chapter 18

It's All You

You Are the Architect of Your Life

Honoring yourself begins with recognizing how truly powerful, potent, and magical you are.

To understand that, you have free will—free will to create the life of your dreams.

All you have to do is choose it.

But sometimes getting from "putting it out there to the Universe" and really recognizing that you control your destiny is a total leap. Sometimes, it's one little choice at a time, and other times, it feels like a big leap to make a different choice.

As I stepped into my personal power, I had to disengage from the old patterns of feeling like a victim in my life or playing pathetic. Believe me, I spent most of my life feeling like a victim, so I'm well qualified to discuss this with you.

I am a pleaser or an "obliger" in Gretchen Rubin's *Four Tendencies* personality test. It's one of the reasons co-writing works so well for me. I'll work harder for someone else than I will for myself.

But that also meant

I was waiting for someone else to recognize my greatness.

To discover me. I had a bit of the rescue fantasy.

Are you waiting for someone to discover your talent? To finally tell you that you're good enough? That you've arrived, even?

Let me tell you—*it won't happen until you honor yourself.*

In relationships, I tend to go passive, deferring to whatever the other person wants. Letting someone else lead. It ties back to my desire to not be wrong or do something judgable. If the other person picks, I can't be held responsible.

Of course, that means I'll probably be secretly or not-so-secretly blaming them if things do go wrong. The energy of blaming is another one I had to heal in myself. I remember noticing how often I blamed my kids for things. Little things, like leaving five minutes late for school. I would let them feel it was their fault for not hurrying up, not getting their shoes on fast enough, etc.

Quantum healer Simone Gers was working with me on this, and she said I needed to have more of the Latin American energy of throwing my hands in the air, shrugging and saying, oh well, things happen. It's no one's fault, it just happened.

That single concept gave me so much more breath and freedom in my life. When I started down the path of figuring out who to assign blame to, I'd remember to shrug and think, it happened. But my desire to blame had been woven tightly into wanting to be right. Afraid to be wrong. Needing to be perfect, correct, blameless. The good girl who never messes up or makes mistakes.

If I was so afraid of being wrong, then you can see how important it would be to assign blame to someone else. And if things didn't go my way, to play victim to them rather than believe I had created the situation with my choices.

In psychology, they talk about individuals who have an internal or external locus of control. Those with an internal locus believe that the outcomes of their actions are results of their own abilities. Those with an external locus of control believe life is happening to them—that their successes or failures result from external factors beyond their control, such as luck, fate, circumstance, injustice, bias, or teachers who are unfair, prejudiced, or unskilled.

The individuals who believe they control their lives tend to be more successful in life.

I seriously think every self help book out there aims to help readers understand they control their own destinies.

The law of attraction states that the vibration in which we dwell (our thoughts and beliefs) shapes and attracts our reality.

Have you ever noticed how angry this concept makes people? They don't want to believe they would be responsible for creating something less than perfect. If they're caught up in thinking there's a right and wrong, then that would make them wrong!

It's especially difficult to understand in ugly situations like with abuse or illness. It smacks of victim-blaming. If someone has cancer, to think they chose it on some level seems offensive. If someone was born to abusive parents, did they choose or attract that energy as an infant? How could an infant choose illness or abuse?

Tanner Gers, my Quantum Shaman Simone's son, lost his vision in a car accident when he was twenty-one. When he was in ICU in a coma, his head as big as a basketball, she plastered the walls with pictures from his life, so every person who came in the room would see him at his best. When people came to Tanner's ICU room to visit, the first thing she said to them was "Come in! Doesn't he look great!" She knew that others' capacity to see Tanner vibrantly alive and looking great even though in the moment it didn't look good at all was one of the keys to his recovery. She watched the confusion in their faces as they tried to shift from *oh shit this is horrible* to *okay, I'll go along with her*. Because of her capacity to hold the power of Tanner's soul, she knew she was the best mom for him. That didn't mean that she didn't have moments of fear, but she was fearless within the circumstances.

Months later when Tanner was home recovering from a broken back, traumatic brain injury, dealing with blindness, and having lost one third of his body weight, her husband came home to her son in an especially low state of mind. When asked what was wrong, Tanner said something like "Don't you see. I'm blind. I'm weak. My life is over." And her husband replied something like "yes, you're blind. But you're not blind and deaf and a quadraplegic. You've got so much to live for. Chin up. Let's live." And he did. One choice at a time. He went on to become a Paralympian in track and field, a champion cyclist, a hall of fame baseball player, earn three degrees, become a father, and an author. He chose life.

One thing I choose to remember is that I'm an infinite being. And so is every other person. I came into this world to experience things and make choices. We all do. Within every experience, there are infinite choices, even though we sometimes see so few. Choices from fear, from anger, from victimization, abuse, from guilt, shame, from joy, from hopefulness, from love. They're all available to us.

You may have come here in this reality to face abuse, illness, or trauma and choose out of it. To say *never again*, which also helps others to be able to choose out of it as well. Or to choose you instead of self sacrifice. To choose to experience success this time around.

It helps to understand the energies of abuse, illness, trauma exist all around us on this planet. When we live by default, not believing we have conscious choice, these energies can adversely affect us. Or we can create something greater.

When I was sixteen, my brother was diagnosed with schizophrenia after a suicide attempt. At the time, I felt like a victim of it all. It seemed unfair. I was angry at the doctors for giving him this diagnosis that I didn't believe. I was mad at my mom for the way she tried to navigate what I now realize was a very difficult road with almost no social support.

But now, with the perspective of choice, I can see how maybe we weren't all at the affect of a merciless God. I now believe my brother, who is fully-functioning in society, chose to experience mental illness in this lifetime to be a part of the change for acceptance and advocacy for the mentally ill. That's a much more empowered and empowering thought than believing that he's a victim of schizophrenia, and I, as his sister, am also a victim of it (which is certainly how I felt at the time).

Think about it. When I see my brother as the powerful being who chose to experience something for his own soul's growth and to assist humanity, my perception and energy lift both of us up. My belief changes everything–for him and me. Research shows us that through quantum entanglement, patients' healing is positively impacted by doctors who have positive outlooks, who believe they can heal and have a great life. You don't want the doctor to lift your chart and think something negative before walking into your room. Think about how powerful you are each time you choose to write. You have the choice to think *I'm a great writer. I love writing. My life is so amazing. I love this book, and it's going to be a great success! I love that my book is going to contribute to readers' lives. Wow! I'm a powerful creator.* And then start writing. What a powerful place to write from. You get to choose what you believe every time you write.

Feeling helpless, like you have no control, is terrifying. Fear is one of the worst energetic places to choose from. The thing is, you do have control of your next choice and the energetic place you make it from. I'm not saying this is always easy. What I'm saying is you have a choice. Sometimes, you may need a moment to acknowledge everything that comes up. Acknowledge it all. Maybe contemplate in your journal. Always know, though, that you can choose from your place of power. Often we put pressure on ourselves in the moment to choose now! And right now, you're afraid. Breathe. Give yourself the space you need to get back to the mindset that you are a powerful, awesome being, and you choose from that place.

If you believe you have choice in everything, you can completely transform your life. What if you believed you could choose for millions of people to read your books? That Amazon would get your book out of content review or the erotica dungeon or whatever current bump in the road you've hit? If Facebook shuts down your ad account, do you believe you can choose to have it reinstated with total ease?

Can you take yourself to the energetic place where it's already reinstated, and more and more people are clicking buy now? That place already exists, waiting for you to choose it.

Anything is possible if we choose to believe it.

It's so important to remember that you have choice. You may have been living by default because you were conditioned to work hard, to have low expectations, to not acknowledge your gifts, and didn't realize how truly powerful you are. But now you know! You can change anything!

In a way, it seems like this step should have been the first one, and yet I have it as the last. But sometimes you need to witness how you've changed things, how the Universe responds to your requests. Manifests your desires, to believe you are the master of your own Universe. If you think of these steps not as linear, but as a circle you repeat again and again, then you'll see how after truly completing this one–honoring yourself by believing you are a powerful being with choice who creates with your thoughts, feelings, and energy–then you're truly prepared to slay. To topple the world and change this entire reality simply by the realization of your dreams.

Honoring Yourself Changes Everything

This step is about *treating yourself* like a millionaire author. That means putting yourself at the top of the list. Prioritizing you. So many of us are pulled in many directions. You have kids to take care of, aging parents, maybe a spouse or partner, pets. If you're not working another job, you might be the one with the flexible time schedule. So people won't understand why you can't drop everything to serve their needs.

This step may not seem that important. Who cares about your needs? You're just going to keep working hard and pushing forward. Once you're rich, then you can sit back and enjoy the fruits of your labor. Right?

Wrong.

Honoring yourself is an integral part of pulling in abundance. It sends a powerful message to the Universe of how you deserve to be treated. Remember my story about visiting Miraval and feeling less-than? When you don't prioritize your time, career, and energy, you're telling the Universe you're not worth it. That it should come out and shame you for not parking your car straight between the lines.

We want to let the Universe know how we expect to be treated–with honor and respect. *Like a freaking queen!* And we do that by treating ourselves with honor and respect.

This means:

- Setting appropriate boundaries, including honoring your writing time
- Taking care of your body
- Not contorting your schedule or your time for others
- Not taking care of everyone else until you've taken care of yourself
- Noticing where you put others first

When my co-author, Lee, had her second baby, she was run down and exhausted. She had two nursing children, was writing and marketing her own books, and hadn't had a full night's sleep in months.

Parenting little ones is intense. It's extremely difficult to put yourself first when your babies literally can't do anything for themselves to even survive. She barely had the time and focus to give her books and her author career, and she certainly couldn't prioritize taking care of her body, even though it was complaining loudly.

That was about the same time I had committed to regular frequent workouts as absolute musts for my body and my mental health to get me through my divorce. After watching me make it a priority, Lee decided to dedicate the next month to her own well-being. She deemed it "a Month of Me". She booked herself a massage and a facial and committed to regular yoga classes. She also asked the Universe to help her figure out how to spend more time with her new baby and still have her career work.

That month, by focusing on herself and her own well-being, magic happened.

She chatted with her author friend, Stasia Black, about an old dark mafia romance trilogy she'd written—her first published books. Stasia offered to take a look at them with the idea of possibly co-authoring with her to rewrite and remarket them.

The trilogy became Lee's all-time best-selling books. Stasia did the bulk of the work in re-tooling them, and then they invested big in Facebook ads, which, again, Stasia took the lead on. They made a killing on the trilogy. Seriously—a killing—and went on to write a second three-book series.

It was the miracle Lee had been asking for—time with her babies while still having success in her career. By making herself a priority, she opened the doors to receiving.

It wasn't something she could have planned or even knew to ask for.

She didn't push against the energy she wanted–she didn't kvetch and complain about how impossible it is to be a new mom and maintain a career. She didn't fight her situation. That would put her in the energy of lack, which we know creates more lack. Lee asked for help and made herself a priority.

Abundance flowed. It came quickly and easily and from a totally unexpected direction! It was her best summer ever. She put herself first on her to-do list, and didn't really think of business.

Like many authors, I had a day job when I started writing. I also had small children. I made a practice of writing in the in-between times. I would write on my laptop during the thirty minutes of swim lessons. On my phone at the playground. In bed at night after the kids went to sleep. Now, ten years later. I find myself still contorting my schedule around theirs. My children are teenagers. They don't need me to do these gymnastics, but I've made it a habit. Instead of prioritizing my work, which is a multi-million dollar business, I'm still worrying about driving kids to school, picking them up, taking them to the mall or to Starbucks for a treat.

Of course, many of these things I absolutely enjoy, but it's important that I examine all my commitments and make sure I'm actively choosing them and not acting out of default. Not out of a learned behavior of putting everyone else's needs before mine.

I need to remember to prioritize my writing and my career because other things can flex too, not just me.

Case Study: Rebecca Hefner / Ayla Asher - It's Raining BookBubs!

Author Rebecca Hefner writes paranormal and sci-fi romance as well as contemporary romance under the name of Ayla Asher. With both pen names combined, she's published twenty-two books in three and half years.

"My main money block was I gave everything away for free–I'd just give away signed copies of my book instead of selling them."

This is a common block that stems from a sense of kindness and generosity. My ex-husband functioned from this space. When abundance came to him, he was quick to share it, which means it doesn't usually stick around. Of course we want to be kind and generous, but we also have to value ourselves, our work, and our time.

One of the things that helped mitigate Rebecca's urge to give away her books was setting up an online store where readers can purchase signed copies directly. "The store has been great because it's a buffer between me and the reader."

Rebecca is the administrator of a Facebook group for authors who want information on marketing audiobooks wide. Through that group, she was offering one-on-one consultations with other authors for free. "I'm happy to do it–I want to help everyone," she explained.

"A few weeks ago, I had a fellow author from our [Author Abundance Facebook] group gently tell me after I consulted with her that she was observing some money blocks with me." Rebecca realized that not charging for her time was a dishonoring of herself and had an effect on her abundance.

"I've always been a believer in manifestation, meditation, expressing gratitude, setting intentions, etc., but...this really resonated and led me to join your abundance Zoom live last month instead of listening at night as I usually do."

Showing up for the call was all it took. "It was awesome, and I felt some things shift inside. I think becoming aware of it was a good step."

Following the call, Rebecca was accepted for not just one but two (one under each pen name) BookBub featured deals and a Chirp deal in the same week **after going almost three years without one.** She said, "I started doing that work and *voila*...**it's raining BookBubs!**"

"My first thought was, *I wonder if BookBub is broken, and they sent me these acceptance emails by accident...* but I realized it's probably a manifestation of the work I've been doing, much of which was generated from your abundance group."

For a moment, she started to go into contraction, wondering if she should re-read the books that were accepted, in case they weren't good enough, but she continued clearing her blocks. "I have to trust that it's going to work, and I will attract the right readers."

Chapter 19

Include Your Body

Your Body Can Attract Abundance

Would you believe that your body is actually part of your team when it comes to attracting abundance or manifesting what you desire?

Here's the thing—abundance doesn't really benefit our beings. It benefits our bodies. It indirectly benefits our minds because it takes the stress out of many situations, but for the most part, the main recipient of your abundance will be your body. Your body is what will receive the benefit and glory in having luxurious things. It will be the recipient of driving a nicer car, living in more comfortable surroundings, and eating better food. So it makes sense that your body should be included in the creation process, doesn't it?

A few of you know that I am a bodyworker. In addition to several energetic modalities, I have a four-year certification in Feldenkrais Method®, a somatic therapy that uses the nervous system to bring the body into better alignment and ease. One of the things they taught me in my training was to NOT separate body from being. When we describe

265

movement or body placement, we're always supposed to say "you" not "your body."

However, it wasn't until I started treating the two like separate energetic entities that I was able to make headway with working with my body. You've heard of intuitive eating? Well, the messages can be confusing if you're trying to tune in but don't know who you're listening to. For example, I'd try to check in intuitively about what to eat for breakfast. The problem was that my brain wanted the comfort food (cereal) while my body was asking for something healthier (smoothie), and since I was hearing both, I couldn't figure out which to follow. Having two choices made it easy for me to talk myself out of the healthier option. Once I got clear on addressing my body as a separate entity, I got clear answers. I also stopped (well, I'm a work in progress, so I made progress on) bullying my body. Treating it with more kindness, honoring, and allowance instead of expecting the world of it and getting pissed when it doesn't deliver.

Using the Body to Manifest our Desires

The body actually acts like a guide or guardian angel when it comes to manifesting and creating your best life. You probably already know you can use your body to get information about situations (what we call following your gut instinct), but you can also use it to attract and receive abundance.

The body will act as a magnet to draw to you what you desire. How? Give it the job. Make it part of your team. Listen to it. And most of all... BE KIND TO IT.

If you're not paying attention to your body, not giving it what it needs or deserves, and not listening when it talks to you, you won't be aligned with it to make this magic happen. I know when I bully my body, push it too hard or ignore it, I end up feeling disconnected from source energy.

If you don't make a practice of listening to the messages from your body, you can't use it to hone in on that "gut instinct" about things. Your body is your primary intuitive conduit. If you've disconnected body from brain, you could be missing out on information that could make your author business flourish.

So, my dear rock star authors...What are some easy ways you can employ the magic of your body?

Home Play

Ask your body what it wants to eat before your next meal and trust whatever shows up in your mind. If you're at a restaurant, try asking your body first, then scanning the menu to see where your eye is drawn. When I have followed this method, the food I ended up ordering—food I would've normally written off as not on my diet, or not of interest—has tasted so incredibly good that it made my whole body light up.

- Take time for movement—ideally an hour a day. Any kind of movement works—whatever your body likes.
- Notice when it protests. Have you been sitting too long? Do you have to pee, but you've been making your body wait? Are you thirsty? Your body is there for you—it's time for you to show up for it.
- Tune in and ask your body if there's something special it requires (massage, acupuncture, a

doctor visit, a spa visit, etc) and then make arrangements to give it to yourself.

- Tune in and ask your body where it wants to work. Maybe one day, it wants to be outside. Another day it may be in the comfy chair. Another day it may be in front of a beautiful view or in a coffee shop you love.
- Ask your body if it likes the space you call your office. If no, ask it what it would like. Maybe it wants a new paint color or to rearrange the furniture.
- Set up your desk or workspace for optimal alignment and ergonomics. Get the wobble chair or the pricey ergonomic office chair. Invest in a stand for your laptop, so you're not looking down and straining your neck. Use a remote mouse and keyboard. Your writing is your craft, and if you're not comfortable doing it, it will take a toll.
- Journal on the contemplations: *What are all the ways I could take care of my body? What would my body like to do for movement?*

Sex Creates Abundance

Whaaaaaat? I know what you're thinking: Renee, you've definitely gone too far now. We knew you were a smexy author, but this is just too much.

Okay, if you're feeling prude, skip this section.

If you can hang, I have another tidbit for you.

Sex creates.

Think about it—the very act of sex is to conceive. There's also a sexual turn-on to abundance. Why do you think those billionaire romances sell so well? It's not just the power that money conveys. Money is sexy to us.

I first had this pointed out by a client of mine who was telling me about having dinner with another couple. This couple, she explained, got turned on by money. They loved to talk about it at the dinner table, brandish it about. It was almost their kink.

I'd seen that before on a documentary about high-end fashion. The woman said often couples came into the high-end department store to buy clothes...*as foreplay*.

Hey, I've used it in a romance novel or two!

If you're feeling adventurous, take a moment and tune into your body. Now, imagine an enormous sum of money coming to you. Notice where in your body you feel it. Close your eyes and really tune in.

What did you observe? A warmth in your heart center? A fullness in your chest? How about a tingling between your legs? Was there a bit of a turn-on to having that abundance?

In our society, sexualness is taboo. My calling attention to the sexualness of money feels taboo. But it isn't wrong. We've just been conditioned to feel it's wrong.

I only call your attention to this in case you're cutting off the possibility of abundance because you suppress your sexuality in general. Would you be willing to let money turn you on?

What if sex was actually the magic sauce you required to pull in the money? And hey, you don't need a partner for it. What if you just had your own million dollar masturbation session? Only you know how you'd like this to look, but what if you pictured your manifestation goal right before or after you orgasm? Orgasm lights up all the pleasure centers in our brains and floods the body with feel-good chemicals.

So you'd be linking all that feel-good juice with the thoughts and images of your desired creation.

When I think about something I want to manifest, I pay attention to whether I'm turned on or not. If I'm turned on, it shows me that the manifestation is coming–I'm already receiving the abundance of it. If I don't feel turned on, I know I need to raise my vibration and pull it in. *Million dollar masturbation, anyone?*

Chapter 20

Celebrate to Create

T he energy of gratitude is almost the same as abundance, which is why *every manifesting process includes gratitude.*

A lot of times we come at gratitude from a "should" place. We try to force ourselves into gratitude. I think that happens when you're not acknowledging yourself. If you're not appreciating the hell out of you, it can be hard to find anything else to be grateful for, right?

We all have this habit of deflecting our own wins. I've flipped so many successes into failures in my head by telling myself things like "that *USA Today* list hit didn't count because it was with a boxset" or that hitting seven figures in royalties last year wasn't legit because it included co-authored books. I used to have this really stupid idea that hitting high on the charts didn't count if I was advertising. Like I was somehow artificially manipulating the system, and success only counted if people mysteriously found my books without me pointing them there! As if only word-of-mouth advertising was legit, and everything else was throwing the game.

All of those minimizations of success kill the magic. Magic happens when we tell the Universe, YES! I DID THAT! IT WAS AWESOME! I AM AWESOME! I LOVE SUCCEEDING! That energy tells the Universe you want more of that success. That you loved it, you're flourishing with it, and to please bring you another heaping dose.

The more you celebrate every win, the everyday ones like writing a thousand words, figuring out the next piece of your plot, sending out your newsletter, the more easily things will flow for you. Pat yourself on the back a hundred times today and watch how you start to create everything with total ease.

Make it your new, most important habit. Acknowledge the hell out of yourself, all day, every day. Associate feeling good with your successes and wins. Don't just move onto the next target without really acknowledging how amazing it is that you hit your current one. Bypassing, not allowing yourself to fully receive success, sends the message to the Universe that you're still not good enough, and that's what will show up for you.

Don't be afraid celebrating your wins will "go to your head" or you'll stop improving or get lazy. I believe it will be the opposite—you'll clear out all the resistance that was holding you back, clogging your creativity, slowing your roll toward your targets.

Often our wins feel anticlimactic, and that's because energetically, we already had to be there in order to actualize the thing in our life. By the time success shows up, you've already "had it" energetically, and you're zooming onto the next thing. Rushing to the next target can make it too easy to skip celebrations, and yet celebrations are such an important part of cultivating your abundance mindset.

Do you trust that your success is inevitable, and pausing to honor yourself and your achievements will actually create something greater? Are you worth the time and space to celebrate?

How do you like to celebrate? I often forget. I write so many books, it can feel like just another day when I finish one. But marking these achievements is important. Author Jane Henry treats herself to a new pair of shoes every time she finishes a book. Vanessa Vale goes plant shopping.

Author Lisa Daily puts money bag stickers on her publishing planner to show every time she gets paid. When she looks at her planner and sees it's covered in little green stickers it makes her feel abundant.

I recently hit the *USA Today* bestseller list with two books in the same week. I've now hit over a dozen times, so it might be easy to let it slide without any fanfare. I no longer crave it as proof that I'm good enough or that I've arrived. Okay, maybe I do still have a bit of that, but I'm trying to clear it!

I know that hitting is still special, still worth celebrating. I still need to fully receive the awesomeness every time it happens to affirm that I want more of this type of success. More bestsellers. More list-hits, more, more, more.

So when local author Tess Summers called me up to say, "How are we going to celebrate your list hit?" I didn't brush it off. We made it into a party, getting together with several other local authors at a bar to toast to the joy.

I should point out how great it is to have this local group of authors who are willing to cheer me on. Authoring can be a lonely biz–be sure to find a posse who will lift you up and celebrate your wins with you. If you don't have one now, set the intention, and those friends will show up.

If you're in a mastermind group or an author group of

any kind, try making the sharing of wins a part of your regular routine. In one 7-Figure Mastermind group I'm in, we take the time at the beginning of the meeting to do this, and it adds the energy of positivity and support that we're there for.

Possible Ways / Things to Celebrate:

- Make a word count celebration for yourself. If you wrote one word or 10,000, they are all still more than you had before. Acknowledge every word you write. You could celebrate daily, weekly, monthly, or all three! Tess Summers likes to set a spa day for herself if she meets a certain word count goal for the month.
- Crack a bottle of champagne for your new release, regardless of whether it's storming the charts. You finished and published a book! That's quite the accomplishment. It's important to really receive how amazing it is that you've already accomplished what most people only dream of.
- Try Lisa Daily's trick of putting money bag stickers on your planner every time you get paid.

The Big Goals

"Yes!" I launched to my feet, both fists high in the air in a victory pump like I was at a sporting event and my team just won the scoring point. Then a moment of doubt overcame me, I sat back down to check my screen again and then surged to my feet a second time for a renewed celebration.

My family laughed at me as I took a victory lap around the kitchen table.

It was a Wednesday afternoon in 2016, and I'd just used that secret back door method of looking up the previous week's *USA Today* bestsellers before they get published the following day.

I'd made the *USA Today* list.

It was a dream come true. Something I felt to my core that I deserved but also desperately needed. You see, I craved that validation. I needed an outside award or badge to affirm that what I was doing—this writing of kinky romance stories—was worthy. I needed to feel like a *real author*. Later that afternoon, my husband at the time said, "What's next?"

I beamed at him. "The *New York Times* list."

He shook his head. "No, that's not what I mean. I mean, what else do you need to feel like you've arrived?"

He was right. It wasn't enough to be published. It wasn't enough to be making enough to pay the mortgage. I wanted it all.

And there's nothing wrong with wanting it all. As Abraham-Hicks, the law of attraction guru says, "You never get it wrong, and you never get it done." We're constantly seeking the next best thing—that's our nature. That's the joy of living and creating, but it's also important to really celebrate what you've already achieved. The more you acknowledge how great you already are—with or without those badges of honor—the more easily those things can flow to you.

For me, believing I'm not enough is one of my core wounds. So making the *USA Today* list as part of an anthology wasn't enough, even though I did it eight times. Then I needed to prove I could make it with a regular book (not part of an anthology). Then, that I could make it on a full-priced book (vs. a $.99 sale book). Of course, RWA won't acknowledge it until you've hit top 50 on the list with a non-anthology book, so I guess it still doesn't count, right?

What's next? Well, the *New York Times* list. Yes. But I'm also enough right now. *You* are enough right now.

It's absolutely okay—beyond okay—*encouraged*—to have targets of hitting every one of these exciting goals. Netflix deals. Tiktok fame. Bestseller lists. Yes! Ask, believe, receive. All of it. Put it on your dream boards, set your intention.

But one of the tricks of aligning your energy with them is to believe you already have them. In other words ***that you're already enough.***

Recently, in the middle of a list-run, I panicked. I had a Bookbub, and my book was on sale for $.99. I had decided to try for the list and had spent a thousand dollars a day on Facebook ads for a few days, but the numbers coming in didn't look good enough to make the list (I was shooting for six thousand sales, minimum). Mid-week, I had to decide whether to keep spending or to pull back.

My energy coach, Katherine McIntosh, advised me to ask the book what it wanted. When I tuned into the energy of the book, I realized the book didn't care whether it made the bestseller list or not, but it *did* want me to believe in it. In other words, it wanted to already be a bestseller in my mind. It wanted to be enough. Or actually, *more* than enough. It wanted to be the cat's meow in my mind. I got the nudge to pull back on spending, but not give up making the list. So I cut back my ad budget and just sent out the energy that my book was already a *USA Today* bestseller or deserved to be.

Unbelievably, with barely over four thousand sales—I made the list!

That's quantum entanglements. That's manifestation. Maybe just plain luck, if you don't believe in energy.

I didn't give up on my book, but I didn't get overly attached to the results, either. Logically, it seemed highly unlikely I would make the list with those numbers, yet somehow I sneaked on!

That's the magic of the Universe at work.

Do I think you need to hit the *USA Today* list to prove you're worthy? Nope.

You. Are. Enough.

You wrote a book! Do you know how many people dream of doing that and never even get that far? You published your book! If you're making more than five figures a year, you're already in the top ten percent of all authors!

Receive the energy of having every accolade you've ever dreamed of having right now—*USA Today* list, *Publisher's Weekly, Wall Street Journal, New York Times*, the Vivian or Hugo or whatever award is given for your genre. You can have it energetically. Just close your eyes and ask to have that energy and feel how it feels. I say something like "Universe, show me the energy of my book being on the *New York Times* list," and then I feel the celebration and glory of that feeling.

If energy isn't your language, use your imagination. Just make-believe. Pretend it already happened. Function as if it already happened. Make decisions based on you being an author who has already become a *New York Times* bestseller, who is already making a million or more a year, who has achieved all the targets you wanted to achieve. Believe they're yours.

And remember—when you hear about or see someone else achieve something you want, say, *I'll have that too*, feel their success as if it is your own instead of going into jealousy, lack, or resistance.

Abundance Meditation: Energy Alignment

1. Close your eyes.
2. Perceive your energy bubble around you, about three feet in all directions.
3. Now expand the energy field until it's as big as the room you're in.
4. Expand it until it's as big as the block you're on. As big as the city you're in. As big as the state or province. As big as the country you're in. Expand until you're as big as the Earth. Now as big as the galaxy. Expand your energy field out a hundred million miles in every direction.
5. Open to receive all the possibilities, all the gifts of the Universe. Invite in the energy of *USA Today Bestseller* for the book of your choice. If this is a target you've already hit, invite in the energy of being number one on the list, or staying there for twenty weeks, or having five books on the list at once—whatever feels fun to you!

6. Ask that energy to come into your field. Invite it into your body, into every cell. Ask it to sync up with your energy field. Look for any place the energy won't sync up—anything that doesn't allow this energy to be yours and ask it to come into harmony or leave.

If you're already geared up to make a list run for a particular book, ask your book what it requires from you, either energetically or in actuality. You may want to freewrite in your journal to make sure you capture the full download of what it needs.

Freewriting: Tap into Your Genius

- List five wins you can celebrate that you accomplished in the last week. They can be small wins or big wins. The more you acknowledge, the easier things get. It's like lubricating the wheels to success.
- What successes and accomplishments have you already had that you can honor and celebrate right now?
- How will you reward yourself for meeting your targets?
- How can you improve as a writer?
- What did you create in the past year you'd like to acknowledge?
- What was awesome, amazing, and what did you follow through on?
- What did you target, go for, and actualize?
- What showed up that surprised and delighted you, magically?

Chapter 21

Drama Destroys

P art of honoring yourself is making space for you. You can't create when the energy of others crowds you.

Authoring can be a lonely, solitary endeavor, and so many reach out to become part of the online author community. The romance community, or romancelandia, is especially vibrant.

It can be incredibly supportive. It also has the potential for toxicity.

There will always be drama. Drama is addictive. It's exciting. For fiction writers, it's our world. We're using tension and drama to tell a compelling story.

But it will also distract you from creating your future. It's an energy drain and suck. It keeps you from what's actually important and puts you in a lower vibration. Remember my story about the client-stealing drama? I was caught up in it, wanting to run around telling everyone, so they would take on my point of view until I heard a voice in my head say, "never tell that story again."

Diving into drama and trauma never creates more. It's

not a space of kindness or allowance, even if you think you're cheering on the underdog.

Check your addiction level to drama–is drama always in your world? Are you a vibrational match for it, so it keeps showing up? When something unfortunate happens, do you rush to post about it on social media? Are you drawn to posts about the latest drama? Think about what that creates. You're telling the Universe you want more bad things to happen. You're putting your energy and focus on something that will drain you dry.

Ask the question: *What does this create?*

If you choose to post about your own traumas or weigh in on the latest drama on social media, before you post, do a gut check. Ask questions like, "Will this post create more [good]?" or "Is this kind? Am I in allowance?" If the answer is no, you're probably in resistance or reaction to something, which doesn't create your future, it can destroy it. If you get a no, delete your post. Even if you think you're "right" or have something to prove, or perhaps especially *because* you think you're right or have something to prove, it usually doesn't create something greater in your life to join the fray. Then again, sometimes it does. Do a gut check, and you'll have the right answer.

The more you just turn a blind eye to the drama going on around you, the less it shows up in your world. These days, I miss all the author drama. I never know what's going on or what the vague Facebook (Vaguebook) posts about bullying mean, and that's totally fine by me!

Drama is a time and energy suck. Think about it—when you were last sucked in by a drama, how much time from your day did that consume? What could you have been doing instead? Having a massage? Finishing your chapter? Downloading your inspiration for your next best seller?

What was the residual effect of investing time in that drama? Did you repeat the story to a friend, spouse, or partner when you could have been celebrating your writing accomplishment? How long did that drama linger in your energy field?

Ignoring drama keeps your focus, time, and energy on what you're trying to create. You won't be distracted by what everyone else is doing. You'll compare yourself less and stay in your own energy, which is the powerful place you create from.

When you celebrate your wins and minimize the losses [problems, drama, injustices], you get more of what you want in life–the good stuff.

Comparisonitis

"No one can make you feel inferior without your consent."
— Eleanor Roosevelt

Jealousy is such a terrible feeling, and it totally blocks us energetically when we go there. The best approach to dealing with it is to use it as a tool to show you that you want more in that area. **When you make yourself small, that's when you feel threatened.**

Someone else's book just hit number one on Amazon, and you feel that pinch of jealousy? See it as the Universe showing you untapped potential in yourself. You're in resistance to something you want. You want to be number one, too. Instead of setting your intent and trusting that you'll get there, you go into lack about it. That person has what I want.

Here's my favorite pro-tip any time you notice someone

else experiencing what you'd like to have yourself. Just tell the Universe, "I'll have that too, please." This **pulls the success energy in rather than pushing it away**.

When you see a post about someone's 7-figure movie deal, say "Universe, I'll have that too!" When you notice your author bestie's new release is doing better than yours, celebrate the win as if it were your own. Really feel her success as your own. That tells the Universe you'll have more of THAT (even if THAT wasn't actually your personal victory). It puts you in the receiving mode instead of blocking your abundance. Their win is your win. It's all energy. You can have the energy of it right now. That will bring the physical actualization of it into your life.

Conversely, any time you say "Why not me?" or "Why her or his book?" and you go to jealousy, you reinforce that you don't have it. That you're in lack. I won't pretend I haven't felt it a million times. I have. I do. But more and more, it gets easier to choose to celebrate the wins of everyone around me (whether I know them or not) in order to tell the Universe I love that outcome.

When I first started publishing in 2012, I found it so interesting how riled up and judgmental romance authors got when talking about E.L. James and the *Fifty Shades Trilogy*. Clearly, her meteoric success tweaked people, and not in a good way. So much debate about the merits of her writing, the actual story, and the depiction of BDSM. There was so much controversy around it, particularly amongst the kink authors (which is where I fell).

Rather than having the *high water floats all boats* mentality–and truthfully, I think *Fifty Shades brought* the high water for the rest of us to float on–people were eager to poke holes in it. There was the element of jealousy over her success and a bitterness that the same success hadn't dropped in everyone's lap. In fact, bringing a huge heaping of *gratitude* to James and *Fifty Shades* for opening the door to erotic romance to so many readers would have energetically lubed the pathway to abundance for them.

I saw a similar reaction to sci-fi Author Brandon Sanderson's incredible fifty-million-dollar Kickstarter project. Some people were enthusiastic about what he proved was possible, but for many, it seemed to be triggering. People seemed almost angry at his success, like they were stomping their feet and yelling "Why not me"? As if it made them feel less-than, and they had to compensate by criticizing the whole idea.

Competition is an old energy—one that humanity is ready to evolve beyond. I like to think that comparison was originally a survival tool. When we were cave people, we needed to fit in and be just like everyone in our tribes to survive. We were using comparison and making ourselves like everyone else to not get eaten by wild animals and to find enough food to eat.

That instinct is what makes us feel agitated and unsafe when we compare ourselves with others, and in our own minds, we're not measuring up. We think we need to do things the same as the successful authors and then are disappointed if our outcomes aren't the same as theirs. The truth is–you can't and won't have success the same way they created it. You're not here to be someone else, to live someone else's life, to write someone else's stories. You're a unique being. Your books are unique creations. You will have success in your own way, and comparing yourself with others only blocks that path. Being the most YOU can be is what harnesses your potential.

I used to go to book signings a total bundle of nerves. I was convinced that I was doing them wrong. Everyone else did them better. There was some secret or formula I hadn't figured out yet, and once I did, they would get much easier for me.

My co-author Lee Savino helped me see that the secret formula was just being me. To show up at a signing being the "Renee-est Renee who ever Renee'ed". Having that mindset gave me so much more freedom. I was able to relax and let the Universe make things easier instead of trying to tightly control and judge everything I was doing.

Everywhere you think you need to compare yourself with someone else to get it right, would you be willing to just drop that instinct and turn up your own magic? Brighten your own light? Be more of yourself? You will get there. You will have their success, but it will be in your own way because there's no one else out there like you. Trust that. Use the energy of others' success as a catalyst for curiosity. Try asking your body questions like *how would you like to experience success? What feels successful to you?* Instead of focusing on the way that others' successes manifest, aligning with what success looks and feels like in you.

Let's watch our incredible author friends hit the *New York Times* list or the top 25 on Amazon and say, "I'm having that. Thank you, Universe, for showing me it's possible!" When an author friend gets a Bookbub, celebrate with them! Then after receiving the energy of success in your field, ask your body *what success do you want to experience now?*

Are you ready and willing to leave competition behind? Truthfully, when one of us is successful as an author, all of us will / can benefit. We don't have to be in competition with each other.

Are you ready to hold all of the success you are capable of manifesting? That's the tricky part. We often want huge success, and somewhere in the background, there's a belief that keeps us from actualizing it. So, if as you start enjoying the energy of others' successes and having some of it, pay attention. Lean in if you are challenged. Have the courage to uncover whatever stops you.

I recently was on a call with a friend who told me her husband just made $200,000 in bitcoin in one week! I realized later that I didn't experience even one second of jealousy or dismay or fear that I'd missed out. I got off the call soaring as if I'd made the money myself. Because I really felt like her win was my win! I decided to invest a little myself while riding that high, feeling like I'd already achieved the success they had. I'll let you know when I hit my $200k.

Home Play

1) Identify a few authors who are really killing it in different ways and ask to experience the energy of their success, telling the Universe you'll have it too.

2) Now think about a couple people who can sometimes trigger you—usually someone who's more neck and neck with you, success-wise. Often a friend. Sometimes a "frene-my". Really feel like her every win is yours. Invite her success along with yours. Yours along with hers. Really support her and watch the support flow right back at you.

*As a note, sometimes we're more triggered by people who strongly see us as competition. It's their crap, not yours. Sometimes just realizing that it's not your stuff to deal with helps you shift away from mirroring / matching their vibra-tion, but sometimes you need to cut the ties and find more supportive friends. Shifting your focus off of relationships that don't create something greater is powerful work. You don't have to do anything other than shift your attention and awareness to the experiences and relationships that are creating something greater, for the people and relationships dragging you out of your power will fade away. Be fearless, and watch what flows into the space in your life the energy of those relationships once occupied.

Chapter 22

Stop Judging Yourself (Or Your Books)

You're already perfect. If you picked up this book because you think something's wrong with you, let me put your mind at ease right now. You already have all the ingredients you need. Don't judge yourself.

Judgment is everywhere, and no one judges you more harshly than you. Changing this habit will make the biggest difference in your money reality because it will tell the Universe that you're not a piece of crap (as you've possibly been projecting), and you do deserve all the abundance and success and to have your every dream delivered.

When you're in judgment about your book, you don't trust your instincts, and then you collapse the field of possibilities. You can't see what needs to be done or be objective.

I recently received the rights back to a series I wrote back in 2015. While I loved it at the time, I've obviously grown a lot as a writer in the years that followed. When I cracked open the books to re-read, I cringed over my old writing style and the fact that the books were more erotica than romance.

Knowing this wasn't the right energy from which to re-launch my books, I focused on lifting the judgment off the books, so I could see what they required. I reached out to one of my co-authors, Vanessa Vale, for an objective opinion about how much work I should put into rewriting them before I published.

It wasn't easy. It's far easier to slip into judgment of your books than it is to celebrate them, but now I have a plan for retooling the books (and it isn't hiding them in a box under my bed!). Now, I'm joyfully, lovingly rewriting. Think about a home remodel. When you bought or built your home, you loved it. After time, your tastes change. Remodeling, changing, expanding is part of life. Focusing on the beauty you are creating is more powerful than focusing on the energy of what was in the past.

I've said it before, but I can't say it enough: You have the answers.

 Stop making everyone else right and yourself wrong.

Or vice versa. Either way, your energy is in resistance to something. You don't have to justify your choices. They just are your choices. You may not like someone else's choice, and it's okay that you would choose something different. You don't have to make someone else's choice wrong to choose something different.

Stop looking for all the answers outside of yourself. Be open to your answers showing up. Yes, they might show up through an expert's opinion or teaching on a certain topic, some inspiration you get from something you see, but you're ultimately the one who knows whether their method will work for you or not or how you're going to use it. You'll know if you get excited about it. If it feels fun and easy. If implementing it flows smoothly.

If you're beating your head against a wall trying to master something the way someone else told you to do it, maybe stop and take a moment to ask what you actually know about _____ (making Tiktok videos, writing ad copy, choosing covers, translating books). Don't just stick with what you *decided* or *concluded* is the way to do it. You have to stay open, to be in question, to follow the first six steps from this book, so you can really engage with the magic of the Universe to create things with ease and flow.

Homeplay

Start noticing all the places you're judging or not trusting yourself. Replace all the judgments with questions instead (but not "why" questions!). Ask the questions and be open to the answer coming in the perfect time, or try freewriting on them, preferably first thing in the morning when your subconscious is open, allowing the Universe to jump in and help you. For example, instead of "I'm so slow, I can't seem to write more than 500 words an hour," flip it into a question:

- Body, would it feel good to write faster?
- How could I write faster with total ease?
- How could it be more fun to get my word count in?
- How can I celebrate the words I actually got on the page?

Instead of "Why can't I grow my royalties enough to quit my day job?" Try asking:

- What can I do or be to bring in a full-time income from writing?
- What am I *unwilling* to do or be to bring in a full-time income from writing? This question can uncover any blocks or resistance or hidden agendas you might be functioning from.
- What would it take to make enough money from my books to quit my job? Universe, show me.

Instead of "My book releases never do well for me," try asking questions like,

- What would it take for this to be my best book release yet?
- What does my book release require to hit ____ target?
- What energy do I need to be or have for this to be my best book launch yet?

Notice I said *yet,* not *ever,* because we want them to keep building. And of course, I want to also acknowledge that growth isn't linear. Some books do better than others, and they still have their place in your portfolio as a whole!

Freewriting: Tap into Your Genius

Freewrite on the following:

- Where (and when and with whom) are you not honoring your time / honoring yourself?
- Where (and when) are you judging yourself, being hard on yourself, or not valuing yourself?
- Where (and about what) do you put high expectations on yourself that are not possible or that you weren't going to do anyway?
- When did you expect yourself to meet linear requirements or perform in a prescribed way in order to fulfill your targets? Could you hit your targets in a new and different way?
- Is there anything you feel shameful about? Would you be willing to clear the judgment around it? Forgive yourself? (See Step One for clearing methods).
- Where are you doubting your own knowing and trying to follow the experts' advice?

- Where are you trying to fix yourself instead of acknowledging how great you already are?
- Where are you resisting your own greatness?

Chapter 23

Be Gentle with Yourself

Let's face it–no one is crueler to you than you are. Would you talk to a friend the way you talk to yourself? Would you have the same expectations of him or her?

The year my dad died and I filed for divorce, I still had the same expectations for myself–to double my income. Not surprisingly, my income remained more or less flat. I spent the year feeling like I was treading water and feeling disappointed I hadn't managed to double my income as I'd hoped. But at the end of the year, I finally gave myself some grace.

I acknowledged I'd gone through a lot and simply maintaining my income level for the year was an accomplishment in itself. When I hear friends of mine beating themselves up because they can't write through a parents' death or in the middle of a pregnancy or a divorce, I remind them that they are processing a lot. Just showing up and making it through the day is amazing.

The truth is, the more you take care of yourself in those difficult times, the faster and easier it will be to bounce back when your energy and focus have returned. And maybe, like when Lee took care of herself with the birth of her second baby, you'll call in your best year ever if you allow the Universe to contribute.

When I first separated from my husband, I couldn't stop crying. I got on a Zoom with Katherine McIntosh, my energy coach, and apologized for not being able to stop enough to even get it together to tell her what was going on. She asked me the question, "How long do you need to cry? Five days? Five weeks? Five months?"

My gut said one week. She told me to give myself permission to cry for the week. To let it out and not judge it.

It seemed like radical advice. I didn't have to pull myself together and try to push through like things were normal? I didn't have to swallow down the tears?

I took her advice and let myself cry. I also let myself experience the anxiety of being alone for the first time in my life. Every time I felt anxious, I sat down, put my hand on my chest and leaned into it. Instead of resisting and fighting the anxiety, I allowed it to come out. Interestingly, I discovered it often resolved in less than thirty minutes, when in the past it would've plagued me for months at a time.

The crying lasted five days. That's all.

Because I allowed myself to simply move through these emotional expressions without judgment or resistance, they were no longer lurking inside, taking up brain space, affecting my nervous system, or otherwise eating away at my well-being. I wasn't in resistance to the pain and grief that wanted to pour out. I let it flow without filtering or judging.

By giving myself permission to cry for five days and not holding my feet to the fire on anything but that, I moved through the trauma quite quickly. I felt tired afterward, and a bit empty, but much, much clearer.

In the past, my instinct would've been to try to control the tears. I'd fear "wallowing" or getting depressed. I would fight it or try to fix it. When my mom died, I was so afraid of that, months later, the grief was still stuck in my throat. Simone Gers, my quantum healer, told me to go ahead and express it–that my tears were a tribute to my mom, not some failing at keeping it together.

When we give ourselves grace, when we are gentle and kind and nurturing during the times we believe we're not measuring up, it's easy to move through the tougher times and get back on track. Not only back on track—to rocket forward.

When you're feeling less than accomplished, take a look at what you *did* do, not what you didn't. You didn't get your words in because your pet had an emergency, and you spent the day at the vet? Acknowledge that you're an awesome pet parent, and you prioritized taking care of a loved member of your family.

Take the tiny wins.

Spent the whole day running errands instead of sitting at your desk? Try writing for just fifteen minutes, and then congratulate yourself on showing up. You still moved forward. Acknowledge what you did do.

I know so many authors who struggled during the pandemic. Having kids or a spouse at home threw most of us who normally enjoy a quiet house during the day for a loop. It's a perfect example of a time to just lower expectations. It wouldn't be kind to still expect ourselves to function at full speed.

One tip for giving yourself latitude and understanding when you're not functioning at full performance levels is to ask, *What would I say to a friend who was going through this situation?* and then turn the advice back on yourself.

Honor Your Time–Hire Help!

This is a really hard one for me. Hard work and keeping my nose to the grindstone were instilled as a value by my family lineage. Even now, I feel guilty reading a book for my own pleasure because I feel like I should be writing my own books instead.

I resist hiring the help I need until things get way beyond the critical level. Some of my limiting beliefs around it are:

- It would take me just as long to explain to someone else how to do it as it would to do it myself. This may be true in the short term, but it's very short-sighted. Once they know how to do it, I never have to explain or do it again.
- I can do it myself.
- I'm not afraid of hard work.
- I know how to do it better.
- I don't have time to manage someone else.
- I might hire someone and then not have enough work for them
- I might hire someone, and my royalties dry up, and I can't keep them employed.
- I might have to fire someone, and I don't like confrontation.

Underneath all of that is actually that core wound of mine: I'm not good enough. I'm not worthy of having hired help. There's also a little of the money wound in there. I don't identify as the boss bitch, I identify as the worker bee.

How freaking stupid is that? I'm making seven figures a year–you'd think I could value myself and my time enough to honor myself with hired help.

Bottom line–you're worthy of having help. You're worth it. Your time is worth honoring. Your sanity is more important than doing it all. Get help.

Please, read that again.

Get help anywhere you need it.

Don't just dismiss this section because you think you can't afford it, or you're not there.

Help may just mean a babysitter for a few hours, so you can fill your creative well with some "me time". It may mean a housecleaner. Getting a one-time yard cleanup with a landscape company. It might mean farming out one marketing task. Is there some aspect to your author career that you don't like doing? Please–get help. There might be someone who loves doing it! There might be someone in your author group who loves doing what you hate but hates something you love. Trade. You don't just get your time back, honoring yourself does so much more. Doing something you hate is a drain on your energy. Taking care of yourself gives you more energy to do the parts of your career you love like the writing.

It doesn't have to mean a long-term commitment to an employee.

You could just off-load one task–social media. Or newsletters. Or ads. The person doesn't have to be in the same state or country as you. You might find someone for cheap through Upwork or Fiverr. At the time of writing this book, there is a Facebook group that connects authors to personal assistants: called Author PA Meet & Greet: https://www.facebook.com/groups/628826870633445

I also highly recommend the Tim Ferris book *The Four Hour Work Week* for ideas of how to use a virtual assistant and for inspiration on getting out of the solopreneur rut.

Being a people-pleaser, it took me a while to really grasp that the person I hired was there to help me and not the other way around. When I was thinking about who to hire, my thoughts were around, "Who needs the extra money?" or "Who could I help out with this job?" rather than who was the best fit for me.

My first attempts at hiring people were not great. I let my first translators push me around and squabble with editors. It was absurd. I also literally contorted myself for my first PA, trying to find work she would find fun, versus work I needed the most help with. I was so unwilling to be the boss bitch, or even just the boss. I guess I was trying to show how cool a boss I was.

It worked better for me at first when I hired people who already knew how to do particular jobs for authors– like a publicist, someone who handles my graphics and social media posts, someone who puts together my newsletters, and someone who helps manage my Tiktok posts.

If you're in resistance to getting help, one useful question to ask yourself is, "What would hiring someone free me up to do?" or "What am I losing by not hiring someone?" (Money, time for the things you love to do, sanity, stress.) When you look at it that way, you realize it's crazy not to get help.

Another reframe is to figure out your hourly (or potential hourly) and compare to what it would cost to:

- Have your home cleaned twice a month
- Have someone post your graphics and manage your social media
- Have someone prepare your newsletters / arrange swaps
- Have someone format your books
- Get help with your bookkeeping
- Manage your calendar
- Manage Goodreads
- Manage contests / Facebook parties
- Put together winner goodies for giveaways
- Cross-posting on platforms Facebook, Goodreads,
- Make Tiktok/Instagram videos for you
- Update your website with your new books and bonus content

Check to see if doing everything is tied up in your identity. You pride yourself on handling the household tasks or being able to do it all. You don't want to let go of the old self-image. For me, it was hard to let go of being the PTA mom. I'd taken on that role so firmly. Before my kids were in school, another parent made a strong case for being the mom who is always on campus. The teachers look out for your kids more, and other parents tell you everything that might have happened involving your kid. I wanted my kids to feel like school was fun, and I was a part of it.

But there became a point where I was doing it out of

guilt and the weight of responsibility. Like if I didn't do it, no one else would. My kids grew older and really didn't care if I was on campus or not. I needed to let go of that old identity and put on my millionaire author one instead. There was a sliver of grief involved with the crumbling of the old and stepping into the new. I really did love that identity while it lasted. But I promise, I am even happier now with my new Millionaire Author self-image. And the PTA is still going strong without me. (Sorry, PTA, I hope no one quits as a result of reading this book. I love you with the full depths of my heart and soul).

Problem Seeking

I used to have this ineffective way of solving problems. I'm dubbing it my "Call Three Friends" approach. Any time something went wrong—with my marriage, with one of my kids, with anything in my life—I'd call at least three different friends to get their take on it. I mean, it wasn't an official recipe. It wasn't always three, and I didn't consciously realize this was my predictable approach, but this was the method. Then I'd sort of mash-up all the advice and reflecting I received from my friends and use it to move on. I want to say *move forward*, but I don't believe it actually moved me forward. It just made me feel better about the trench I'd dug to sit in.

For one thing, the more you talk about problems, the more you tell the Universe to bring you more, so the very act of calling three friends was further ingraining the problem. For another thing—*no one has the answer to my problems but me.* Soliciting the advice and opinions of friends or even just telling the story over and over doesn't help.

Getting Help from Your Energetic Team

Everything is energy. We know from physics that even solid objects are made up of tiny, moving particles, and we know from quantum physics that the observer can influence how these particles behave.

Can you believe, then, that everything around you could support you on your journey? You have an energetic team—your helpers who conspire to make things possible, easy, and abundant for you.

You can consciously work with your team and employ their help, which will open you up to more receiving.

Your team could consist of all kinds of energies—your pets, the tree outside your window where you write, your children, your spouse, the entities no longer in bodies, like family members who passed, great parking spots. You might have guardian angels, fairies, tree nymphs, spirit guides, animal spirits, and nature intelligence working with you.

Your houseplants can contribute to your future. Your clothing can contribute to your future. Your garden. Your children—even the tiniest babies—are energetic team members, helping to create your future.

Your body is part of your team! (Another reason to make sure you're honoring it and taking good care of it).

Your books written and yet unwritten are part of your team!

Earlier in this book, I told the story about how valuing myself enough to buy my house made a huge difference in my life. When I moved here, my house became part of my energetic team. It supports who I am and who I am becoming. My Tesla supports my future because it makes me happy every time I get behind the wheel.

Recognizing the significance of the energy of the things

you surround yourself with shows why decluttering and clearing and also treating yourself to luxuries can be a fruitful part of manifesting abundance.

Authoring can feel lonely. Marketing your books can sometimes feel like you're pushing a rock uphill. It helps to know you're not actually alone, that the energies you surround yourself with are all willing and can contribute to your abundance and help you make money.

Children are excellent team members for attracting abundance!

They don't yet have as many fixed points of view about how easily or hard it is to earn money. You can train them to believe what you're not even sure you believe yet. When my children were younger and would make a big request of me (like the ten thousand dollar dinosaur sculpture at the gem show), I would say, "Yes! We can get that when my books make a million dollars". That way, they started resonating with the joy of what would be possible when I was a millionaire author. I was careful not to say "we can't afford that" or project any kind of limitations based on our current reality. I tried to keep it in the realm of what was possible, however outlandish it seemed at the time.

You don't need to do anything special to assemble and receive help from your team, other than acknowledging that you have one. You can include them in your consciousness when you're making your requests of the Universe. I like to just say hello energetically to my kids, pets, car and house, and invite them to help me make money since it benefits us all.

You can also include them when you're asking for guidance. I've heard of people inviting the ghost in their home to bring them a million dollars, or bring them business, or we could invite them to bring us readers. If you want to learn more about connecting directly to your higher guides or to entities, I recommend the books, *Opening to Channel,* by Sanaya Roman and *Talk to the Entities*, by Shannon O'Hara.

Freewriting: Tap into Your Genius

What are all the ways I could receive help?

- Who or what are part of my energetic team?
- How can I open to receive more from them?

Chapter 24

Investing in your Business

T his book is about attracting abundance, not spending it. Right?

Sometimes we are blocked by being unwilling to invest. By holding onto the money we have so tightly, we can't make more.

Don't bring lack mentality to your business–sometimes you need to spend money to make it, and there is a time to invest in your business.

Part of honoring yourself and your career can be investing. This might be in the form of advertising, graphic design, hiring help, buying custom cover photos, or getting your books translated. There are places where spending money will bring a significant return. Don't let your fear of losing that investment or not getting a return stop you.

Your belief that your career is important enough to spend money on sends a powerful signal to the Universe. When you honor your business, the Universe will respond in kind.

When you're considering an expenditure, use the tools

we've honed in this book to access your inner knowing. Freewrite or journal on questions like:

- Will this help me reach new readers?
- Will it make me money?
- Does it create more?

Sometimes you'll get a yes on one but not necessarily the other. For example, when I was trying to decide whether to spend heavy on Facebook ads in order to hit the *USA Today* list for a certain book, I asked if it would make me money and heard no, but when I asked if it would create more, I heard yes. So I understood there might be reasons beyond making a short-term profit to spend to hit the *USA Today* list. As it turned out, the book did hit the list and return a profit, but perhaps it would've returned a better profit without the list. I didn't mind because I trusted the information I received. Hitting the list would create more for my career, and the expenditure was worth it.

I've also found that asking the question, *Will this create more?* helps when deciding where to put my time and effort. For example, I am often invited to write for anthologies. Even though they are distractions from my bread and butter series and rarely make me much money, I more often than not get the nudge to join them. They may not create an immediate monetary return, but they do create more for my career. There might be a connection to another author that blossoms. There might be an intangible benefit like spreading your reach and visibility. Planting seeds for future projects.

If you choose to invest in something for your business, and you're still nervous about it, try using one of the script flips we talked about earlier,

"Every dollar I spend on my business comes back to me tenfold."

Another technique that might bring clarity is to imagine yourself six months from doing it, and how do you feel—heavy or light?

What If Your Investment Doesn't Pan Out?

Let's face it, not every investment in your business is going to have a direct return. Sometimes you spend big, and the return is crappy. It happens. When I was in Kindle Unlimited, it happened more frequently because heavy ad investment was part of the game, and there's a gamble involved. You can't track the return on investment in real time, you're banking on earning the investment back on page reads.

I have had some disappointing losses. Rather than catalog them as failures, though, it helps me to remember that every dollar spent was still an investment in my business. You've heard it said that a consumer needs to see the product advertised seven times before they buy? Well, maybe all that ad spend was setting the groundwork for future books. Next time, readers will see your ad, remember they've seen your name around before, and one-click you this time.

There are no mistakes. Every step you take, every choice you make in your business *does* move it forward. The only thing that keeps it stagnant is doing nothing. Not choosing, not following your gut, not investing, not taking inspired action.

Even if the way forward is learning that the way you just chose is not the way to go again, you've still learned something. You're a different person than the one you were before you made that choice.

Handling Setbacks

Chapter 25

Burnout and Writer's Block

The topic of overwhelm and burnout often comes up in our Author Abundance monthly membership.

We all go through peaks and valleys with our creative output and flow. There's an ebb and flow to all of life, but there are times it feels like you've hit a wall or are stuck. You experience exhaustion, or emptiness in your creative well. The words don't come, or you don't even want to sit down at the computer because it feels forced or like work.

Usually overwhelm isn't about the actual work that needs to be done—you could do that with relative ease. Even ambitious word count goals can be hit with ease with a shift in mindset. Overwhelm is resistance to what you perceive you need to get done, and if that isn't heavy enough already, it's usually piled high and weighed down with a whole bunch of judgment of yourself because you haven't done the task already, are too slow, or think you're somehow failing at it.

Writer's block is a mixture of **resistance plus judgment.**

We put pressure on ourselves to get our manuscripts written, and because that pressure doesn't feel good, we resist the work. Then we judge ourselves for not doing the work. It becomes a negative feedback loop. A perfect storm for never writing another word again. Ever.

Usually, it's your own expectations of yourself that are burning you here.

Perfectionism is a huge culprit. The times I wrote a manuscript thinking I was writing it for an agent vs. when I was writing a book for my fans were completely different experiences. Writing for an agent makes me freeze up. Judge every word.

Look at my work with a far-too-critical eye. Should myself into defeat.

We're taught in today's society to pick ourselves apart. Search for every flaw. I grew up in one of those families where love was shown by pointing out flaws. The idea was we should dust each other off–make sure no one has spinach in her teeth before we went out into the world. I know it was done out of a desire to support and keep me from embarrassing myself, but let me tell you–it didn't produce confidence.

I've heard one of the main causes of hoarding is perfectionism. If the hoarder can't clear things out perfectly, they won't do it at all. I had a roommate in college who described the same thing. She said she either made her bed with a ruler, measuring the sheets on each side to make sure they perfectly matched, or she just left her bed unmade. There was no in-between for her. No quick straightening of the covers to give the appearance of a made bed.

My co-author, Lee Savino, decided it was time to up-level her writing. She was interested in writing rom-com and read a few books on how to best do it. Then she sat down to write her next books and...ugh.

It was painful. Pulling teeth. She barely averaged 1,000 words a day. She resisted writing because she had these huge expectations of herself.

This lasted for almost a year before she found the ticket out: She decided to be *mediocre*. She realized her current fans already love her work. They weren't demanding that she up-level. So she only needed to write books as good as the ones she'd written before.

She just needed to be mediocre.

As soon as she gave herself permission to not be perfect, the words started to flow again. She started enjoying her stories and falling in love with characters again. It all became easy.

And of course, without the pressure of being perfect, she totally up-leveled.

Being critical is crushing. It causes a downward spiral. You lose your belief in yourself, and then you can't perform to your expectations, so you lose more belief. The whole thing snowballs.

It's just like insomnia. One of the main causes of insomnia is...*worrying that you're not sleeping*. It's absolutely normal for humans to wake in the middle of the night. Biologically, we were designed to–perhaps originally to tend the fire in our caves. The problem is, people wake up in the middle of the night and then freak out that they're awake. That freak out keeps them awake... you can see how that becomes a negative feedback loop.

The times I wrote a book for an agent versus writing it for my fans was absolutely agonizing. Instead of indulging in the story, I spent most of the time second-guessing myself, trying to see things through their critical eyes.

There's a time and place for others' eyes–usually during the edit process. Whatever is stopping you from writing, choose to pivot—release yourself from the prison of whatever beliefs, perceptions, or expectations are holding you captive. Choose a different point of view, futurecast, ask what else is possible, get to the bottom of the limiting belief. Choose something different. If it's stopping you from writing, then it has to stop. Here are some other suggestions for moving through stuckness.

Don't Label It

First of all, words have energy. Even though I just put a label on it, *don't.* The moment you start calling it *burnout* or *writer's block,* you solidify the energy. You gave it name, and therefore, form and structure to hang onto. You own it. You hold onto it. The longer you focus on it, the more solid and heavy it becomes.

What if, instead, you could be in the moment with whatever you're experiencing? You could say, "I'm experiencing a bit of exhaustion, but it will pass" instead of "I *am* exhausted" or "I *have* burnout."

When you label something, as soon as you see it as a real thing, you set about proving it to be true. Psychologists call this "confirmation bias". You look for a problem and find evidence it exists.

I've noticed this with my body. When I start saying things like "my metabolism has slowed, and I just can't seem to lose the weight" my body proves me right. The scale will stay stuck on the same number, and nothing I do can change it. But when I clear that limiting belief, when I decide instead that my body feels great, I'm getting in better shape than ever, and the weight just falls off me, I'll lose five pounds in a week and visibly firm up in ways that seem impossible.

Remove the Judgment And Resistance

The second best way to solidify the energy around burnout or writer's block is to judge yourself or your experience. What if it wasn't wrong to hit a wall and require five days of lying on the couch eating bon bons before you can create again? Maybe that's your process. Judging it only makes it not work for you. When you're in allowance of your experience, everything opens up.

Sometimes when I hit a wall, I'll call my friend Simone, and in the natural flow of conversation, the book I'm working on will come up. She loves hearing me talk about my books and my creative process. She will ask me questions from her genuine interest, and as I share with her, I get insights. Space opens up. Who in your circle loves and appreciates you and your work so much, they are delighted to revel in your creative process, to riff with you, maybe even free-talk potential characters or plots or ideas for the future with you? Sometimes, creating out loud with someone can shift everything.

In many cases, it's the resistance to burnout and writer's block that perpetuates it, creating a feedback loop that only strengthens the situation. You feel burnout, and you're scared of burnout, so you push against it, which uses a ton of energy and creates more burnout.

Maybe you're the type of person who pushes hard and then needs to rest. There are seasons to your writing. Is there any reason to fear the resting time? The winter? The farmer doesn't fear letting the land fallow. He or she recognizes this time is necessary to restore fertility.

What if you leaned into the perceived burnout and allowed it to pass? What if you had a conversation with it? Or with your body? "Hello body. How long would you like to rest?" Or with the book you're trying (or resisting) to write? "Hello book! Is there something you'd like me to know?"

> The best way out of what you perceive as burnout or writer's block is to start asking questions.

Try the following as journal prompts or simply close your eyes and feel into the energy for the answers.

- What beliefs do I have about burnout?
- What are the lies I'm believing about burnout? (Our natural state is joy/health/abundance, so if that's not showing up, you've bought into a lie. What is the lie?)
- What am I resisting?
- Go inside your body and ask—what do you require? (Do I need rest, inspiration, a change of scenery, a funny movie?)
- Is this even mine? (Sometimes we take on the energies from others, just like we catch a cold or flu.)
- Is this a problem or a possibility?

If you use EFT, try tapping to the statement, "It is safe for me to write."

Case Study: Jennifer Owenby - Writing Faster

Jennifer Owenby, a member of the Author Abundance monthly calls, uses the Write Faster meditation I recorded before sitting down to write. "I love it. I've been able to release every two months so far this year. It's June, and I'm playing around with a Christmas book, so I'm also ahead of schedule which allows the writing not to be stressful."

She said the meditation helps clear the times when she has no idea what to write next. "Once I'm clear on the story, I'm fine, but I have days where it's like a big cinder block is in my way, and my creative process is pouting in the corner. When I let the barriers down and relax and do the meditation, well I've finished every book BEFORE the deadline since I've been in the monthly abundance calls and using the meditation. Plus, I like to work ahead, so if a book says release me sooner, then I'm ready."

She's also more at peace with writing ahead. "I like having a book or boxset I can release and take time off. I trust my body and brain to just say *nope, time off now*."

Jennifer's income is up, as well. "This last book has

been my best release and best money maker. I hit 356 in the Amazon store. All those meditations are working for sure."

She said one of her blocks to success has been fear. "The more successful you are, the mean authors are coming after you. It's like I want all the success, but I'm curling up, protecting myself from rumors and abuse." Thanks to the monthly calls, she's now actively realizing when she's shrinking. "As often as I can, I lower my walls, expand, expand, expand, then I'm in my safe place with the Universe and receiving all my good, all my help, love, peace, and guidance. Sometimes I do that a few times a day. Sometimes I get busy and forget, but I'm focusing on when I feel myself shrinking and hiding, and I use the tool you gave us."

Chapter 26

Bad or No Reviews

Bad reviews can make you money

Did I get you with that? It's true. Maybe not the way you're thinking or maybe so. Sometimes one-star reviews do help sell a book. I have many savvy author friends who have pulled one-star review quotes to use in ads to promote their books.

But I'm thinking about this from an energetic point of view. You've heard the saying, "There is no such thing as bad PR?" Well, the reason that's true is that all reviews are energy for your book. Bad or good is irrelevant. Only you can shape how that energy affects your book. Hint—it's not through the words of the review, it's through your reaction (or non-reaction) to them.

Gary Douglas, the internationally-recognized thought-leader and founder of Access Consciousness® says that for every judgment you receive without a point of view, or even better, with gratitude, you'll receive five thousand dollars more that year. Conversely, every judgment you resist and react to, you'll lose ten thousand dollars. Why? Because accepting someone's bad review of your book with gratitude puts you in the space of receiving, which is where we want to be to attract abundance.

I love to remember this every time I get poked by a review. I make a conscious decision to flip the energy into a receiving. "Oh! You hated my book? Thanks, that's five thousand more dollars for me!"

Other people's opinions about our books are none of our business, really. I don't know if those exact numbers are true, but I do know my income has soared since I stopped reading reviews. I remember early in my career, *NYT* Best-selling author Annabel Joseph gave the advice to not focus on reviews because you can't control them. Stick to focusing on things you can control like the quality of your books and marketing.

I've always maintained that if I think something's hot, if I love it, someone else will too. Will everyone? Nope. And that's okay. No book is for everyone. Some books may be for a smaller segment of the readers. Some may resonate for a larger segment. There is no right or wrong. No bad or good. Your book is your brilliant creation, and it will find its perfect readers.

When you read a review that upsets you, it creates a wobble in your world. Your resistance and reaction (or alignment and agreement to a good review) can create a positive or negative charge.

Either one tells the Universe that on some level, you believe the person is right, which attracts more judgments/bad reviews. You don't want to send out to the Universe the energy that your book IS flawed (and honestly —isn't every book flawed to some reader? We can't please them all!) because then other readers pick up that energy and see the flaws instead of what's awesome. You don't want to resist and react to any review and create this energetic charge. Instead, practice letting it flow through you or actually nourish you as energy. This doesn't just hold true for bad reviews, but for any judgment. You can practice receiving them with gratitude.

In my online coaching calls, I often start meditations by inviting listeners to drop their barriers and expand out to the farthest reaches of the Universe. This expansion lets all energy move through you without affecting you. If you receive judgments / bad reviews in this space, they can actually energize you. Open up to receive the energy of the review—all reviews. You can even receive the energy of reviews on other people's books if your book lacks reviews. Say "thank you for that judgment" in your most pleasant internal voice. It may feel like sarcasm, but that's okay! You just made gold! You just changed a bad review into money, possibly literally.

Have you heard of Netgalley? It's a place for getting reviews on your books. I splurged $500 (a huge amount for me at the time) to put one of my books in but then panicked about getting bad reviews because the book I submitted was kinky and, therefore, not for everyone. My fear didn't attract bad reviews, but it attracted NO reviews. My book just sat there for several months, receiving only a small handful of reviews. I realized I had shrouded my book or blocked it from being seen. As soon as I saw this, I opened the energy back up and invited reviews in, and then they started pouring in. And they were all good!

Another time, I was releasing book two in my *Zandian Masters* series. It was my first indie KindleUnlimited series launch. I'd gotten the intuition that I needed to get book 2 out as soon as possible to hit that "rapid release" thing with the algorithm, so rather than write another 50K book, like book one, I made it shorter—just 35K and published it three weeks after book one. Good strategy? Totally! One problem —I was terrified everyone would be mad that book two was so short. I brought my fear energy to the release, and sure enough the first couple reviews were complaints about it being too short.

I called up my author bestie Lee Savino. She's a wonderful and unique friend in that she doesn't align and agree with me when I call with a problem (which, face it—is usually what we want from our friends). Instead, she immediately served me a dose of the truth. "You created that!" she said. "You were worried about it, so that's the energy they got. Let it go. The book is fine. Love your book," she advised me. Buoyed, I shifted my energy, recognizing the truth of her words. Guess what? Those first reviews were the last ones I received complaining about length. Everyone else loved the book!

Abundance Meditation: Attracting Reviews

Want to energize your book with reviews?

1. Close your eyes and drop your barriers.
2. Expand your energy out until it's as big as the room you're in. Then as big as your block. Then as big as your city. As big as your state or province. Expand out to fill the space of your entire country. Now the Earth. Now the galaxy. And finally, the Universe.
3. Hold your book in your hands with your imagination or with your physical book—your choice-—they both work the same!
4. Imagine a magnet on your book that draws all the amazing reviews it could possibly receive.
5. Then drop away any point of view about good or bad reviews and just receive the energy of all reviews, tons of eyes and opinions on your book.
6. Feel the energy around your book growing and growing with the more energetic reviews you receive.

7. Send gratitude back out to all the reviews for energizing your book.

Chapter 27

I got kicked out of KU...and I doubled my royalties that year

F irst of all, if you think this is going to be an argument for or against KU, it's not. I don't debate the merits of wide vs Kindle Unlimited because I firmly believe that you have to trust your own gut in your author business. What is right for me may not be right for you. Only you know what will work for you.

Rather, this is the story about how an abundance mindset turns lemons into lemonade. About how thoughts create reality. About the Universe having your back.

When I started self-publishing in 2017, Kindle Unlimited was my bread and butter. Last time I checked, my dashboard showed nearly 300 million page reads, accounting for over a million in royalties. So losing my KU privileges should've hurt, right?

It certainly could have. The first time I was threatened with losing my KU privileges, I nearly puked. I had a permafree book that I accidentally put back into KU before it was down from one of the wide retailers, and I received the form letter saying they were shutting me down. I went into crisis, feeling about as small as a pebble and no more powerful. But I very quickly was able to pivot. I cleared the feelings of shame and impotence and asked the Universe to fix it. When I called Amazon, it was quickly and easily resolved. Ruffled feathers were smoothed, I was not thrown out.

Last spring, though, I was not so lucky.

Or wait–as the story goes–I was terribly lucky! In the same situation as last time, I had a permafree book that I put into KU thinking I'd taken it down from all the places. They contacted me to tell me it was up on a site called Ghandi.mx. Confused, at first I thought it was a pirate site, but it seemed legit. My co-author, Vanessa Vale, helped me do a little research and found out it was one of Kobo's distributors. I contacted Kobo and asked for their help in taking it down. They were very helpful and sent a message to Ghandi.mx. I thought the problem was solved. As it turns out, it wasn't. Totally my fault. Turns out, because it was a permafree book, I'd put it up through Draft2Digital, rather than directly through Kobo, so I was barking up the wrong tree when I asked Kobo to resolve it for me. The next letter I got from Amazon said due to repeated policy violations, my entire library would be removed from Kindle Unlimited.

Rather than crumble into crisis like I had the first time, **I followed my gut, which said this wasn't a problem, it was an opportunity.** The Universe was telling me to go wide.

At this point, my co-written series with Vanessa Vale was wide, and I'd seen how much easier it was to publish without the stress of launching big to tickle the Amazon algorithm. (Again, I'm not trying to convince you of going either way–you know what's best for you!) So I made a half-hearted attempt at changing Amazon's mind, and when they refused, I put my entire catalog wide.

Imagine my delight when I pulled my numbers for 2021. I doubled my income, but my Amazon income was only about 100K more. The majority of my growth for the year–*nearly an additional seven figures*–came from the other retailers. I followed the steps to maintaining an abundance mindset–I cleared negativity, trusted my gut, and opened up to receive–and it paid off.

It can pay off for you, too.

There have been scientific studies proving that people who believe they are lucky *are actually luckier* because they look for and see opportunities that people who think life is out to get them don't.

Abundance mindset can take the pain out of authoring as it attracts greater wealth, joy, and ease to your life.

Peaks and Valleys

Let's face it, success and growth in this business isn't always linear. You don't start at a certain wage and get a pay increase every year until you finally reach your pot of gold. There are peaks, and there are valleys. When you're in the middle of a valley, it's important to remember that it's just a valley. There will be another peak. It doesn't mean you've done something wrong. That your book sucked. Or people aren't reading X anymore. Or that your time is past. Or that you'll never succeed again.

Don't go there. Even the biggest authors have peaks and valleys. It doesn't have to do with the quality of their books. They didn't write better books for the peaks and lower quality for the valleys. There are so many energetic factors at work. When I was studying writing in college, author

Jane Smiley won the Pulitzer, and I remember some of her colleagues saying, "That wasn't even her best book." It may not have been her best book, but it was her time. There's divine timing at work. World events. Reader trends. All kinds of things we can't track. That's why we have to turn the duty of tracking those things over to the Universe and trust our gut. Make our requests. Set our intentions. Follow the breadcrumbs when they're laid out for us.

I often hear stories about authors having an initial surprising success followed by a later disappointment. It might help to dig into the energy of why this might happen. When we first go to publish or to try anything new, we're in a state of hopefulness—we don't have expectations of how it will go because we've never done it before, so we're open to all possibilities. This combination of hope plus being open to all possibilities brings us success. Then we go to release the next book and rather than being in hope and open to possibilities, we have an expectation about how it will go. We think it will go the way the last one did. Expectation closes doors to possibilities. This expectation, this prediction, limits all the infinite possibilities that are available to that book. And so the results might be disappointing.

Trust that the success you've asked for is on its way. You've placed your order with the Universe, and it's coming. If you're open to the magnificence of that success, it'll be there, whether you recognize it or not in the moment. There will be spikes and dips in income. List hits and other book releases with meh results. It's all part of the game, but you're playing a long game. You can weather the ups and downs because you have your abundance mindset now. You trust the Universe has your back and will deliver everything you ask for and allow in.

Case Study: A. L. Jackson - Peaks and Valleys

NYT, Wall Street Journal, and *USA Today* bestselling author A.L. Jackson has been writing contemporary romance for thirteen years. Like many indie authors, her income has fluctuated wildly over the years.

She sold her first book to a small publisher in Australia. "That book sold 50 copies the first year. It was disheartening, but I was learning about the indie world. Ebooks had just come out. I was seeing people have success, and I wanted to do that."

After two books, she bought her rights back from the publisher and went indie.

"The first year I had hardly any success at all. But then my fourth book hit the *New York Times* list and took the first book in that series to the *New York Times* list, too. I had this huge income peak—it was insane. I thought every month was going to be like this."

She accepted a three-book deal with Penguin, but it did not go well. "I got a fairly significant advance, but they didn't know how to balance the indie success with what they were doing. It was very frustrating that it didn't go well. I had all these expectations and promises they'd given me. There were a lot of hard lessons on both sides."

As a result, she experienced a huge dip in income. "I'd bought a new house. That was really scary."

When her three-book deal was complete, she returned to indie publishing. "I love being an indie author, being in control of when I have a sale, the price point, my covers."

Rebuilding took a long time. "It wasn't right out of the gates epic again. A lot of indie authors were experiencing lows at that time as well, but I buckled down and rode the wave."

But then her second book in the new series hit *USA Today*. "I was getting really big dips in income after release, but there was a steady progression. I started using Kindle Unlimited in 2016. I had huge spikes at release and then huge dips in non-release months, but that's leveled as my backlist built."

She realizes there will always be peaks and valleys in this business. "I know I'll have other dips in my career. I've been in it long enough to recognize that. You have to find within yourself what you're doing this for and remember that during the times when it's not easy."

Her advice to other authors is to stay true to your passion. "If you have a burning desire to write, then you're a writer. You have to make that work. Feed that passion with those words when you can. The mindset has to be that you're doing it out of your love for it and because you have to."

Now is your Time

Chapter 28

You've Got This!

I f you stuck with me this long, you've probably already absorbed that abundance mindset can and will change your life. Mindset is everything. It takes away the ache of feeling like what you want is out of reach. It soothes the wounds inflicted by comparisons and perceived failures. It eases the tension and anxiety produced by the belief that you'll get there if you just try harder. Or finally get it right.

There is no right.

You are already perfect.

And you can have it all.

If you follow the seven steps in this book–not as a one-and-done, linear attempt but as a practice–you will manifest all your desires. I can't say when or how. All I know is that the more you believe in yourself–your magic, your potential, your power–the more powerful you become.

This book was designed to light the flame of abundance mentality for you, so you will be open to having the right answers, the right connections, all the magic of the Universe drop into your lap at the right time. When you believe in yourself and your books, when you're open to receiving abundance, that's when the quantum entanglements can work to propel your career to the highest heights.

You will no longer be creating by default–functioning from old operating systems rooted in fear or lack of self-worth. You can now create with intention. Envision the career you want for yourself, invite the energy of that future into your now.

I believe you can achieve all your targets as an author without pushing yourself. You can ask the Universe to assist you and receive that assistance with total ease. You can allow the Universe to deliver in ways you can't even contemplate yet, but you follow your inner guidance, take action when you know you are supposed to, write what you love, market it from the heart, and let the Universe work all its magic to keep you in abundance.

I know you can achieve this vision you have for yourself.

Remember that there are no mistakes–every choice you make will move you forward.

You've got it, and we're here for you. You can harness the magic of the Universe to create this for yourself.

Join the Community

One of the best ways to see abundance in your life is to surround yourself with like-minded people. It's said that energetically, we are the average of the five people we're around every day, so we want to make sure those people are who we wish to be like.

If you're ready to surround yourself with other authors dwelling in possibilities and interested in uplifting others, we invite you to join us in our Author Abundance Central

Facebook. https://www.facebook.com/groups/
authorabundance/

Sign up to receive Author Abundance Affirmations sent straight to your inbox every week! https://www.subscribepage.com/authorabundanceaffirmations

Join the Author Abundance monthly membership for live coaching, energetic clearing, meditation, and discussion of what's possible. https://millionaire-author-coaching.teachable.com/p/author-abundance-membership

Chapter 29

Author Abundance Resources

Join the *Write to Riches* Eight-Week Online Course

Ready to take your Manifesting abilities to the next level?

Deep dive into the *Write to Riches* process with this new, guided, in-depth eight week course.

Simply the act of joining forces with a community of like-minded manifestors can ignite your power to receive, create and generate for your future.

You are standing on the precipice of having it all. Take it. Activate it, keep it. It's yours.

This eight-week course will open your eyes to blocks and limitations you've had in place and help you act. There will be video course work and live weekly Zoom calls as well as a journaling cafe where you can show up and download answers from the Universe for your career.

https://write-to-riches.teachable.com

Author Abundance Affirmations

Sign up to receive a weekly Millionaire Author Affirmation delivered straight from the Universe (via me) to your inbox! These weekly reminders will keep you on track and positive as you become your Millionaire Author self. https://www.subscribepage.com/authorabundanceaffirmations

Write Faster Meditation - FREE

I recorded this meditation to help authors get into the flow and write all the words. You can access it for free here: https://millionaire-author-coaching.teachable.com/p/a-meditation-for-fast-writing

Author Abundance Newsletter

Sign up to get news about live video calls and mindset coaching: https://www.subscribepage.com/abundantauthor

Author Abundance Central (Facebook Group)

Join the Author Abundance Central Facebook group: https://www.facebook.com/groups/authorabundance/

Join the Author Abundance Monthly Membership

The Author Abundance monthly membership provides live monthly coaching calls with me and Lee Savino, along with access to a community of like-minded authors, a library of meditations, hypnosis and tapping videos, as well as recordings of past calls and bonus resources) https://million-aire-author-coaching.teachable.com/p/author-abundance-membership

Books that Changed my World

You are a Badass at Making Money by Jennifer Sincero

Get Rich, Lucky Bitch and *Chill and Prosper* by Denise Duffield-Thomas

Feel Free to Prosper: Two Weeks to Unexpected Income with the Simplest Prosperity Laws Available by Marilyn Jennett

Playing the Matrix by Mike Dooley

E-Squared: Nine Do-It-Yourself Energy Experiments That Prove Your Thoughts Create Your Reality by Pam Grout

The Universe Has Your Back by Gabrielle Bernstein

We Should All Be Millionaires by Rachel Rodgers

The Four Hour Work Week by Tim Ferriss (for abundance of time and lifestyle design)

Excuse Me, Your Life is Waiting: The Power of Feelings by Lynn Grabhorn

Don't Diet, Be Happy by Katherine McIntosh for kindness to your body and including it in your manifestation process.

Being You, Changing the World (for an introduction to the magnificent energy tools I learned from Access Consciousness®

Notes

1. Introduction

1. **A Note about Terms:** In this book, I refer to "the Universe" as a cosmic force that we can ask for and receive from. It's a term that works for me, but please replace it with your subconscious, higher self, God, All that Is, Quantum Entanglements or whatever resonates for you. Like everything in this book, take the tools that work or fit, leave the ones that don't.

4. Money Blocks

1. (https://www.brookings.edu/blog/up-front/2020/11/30/what-are-inflation-expectations-why-do-they-matter/)

Case Study: Alta Hensley - Coming out of the Box

1. *Access Bars® is a gentle treatment using light touch on the head.

12. Receiving

1. https://www.sciencedaily.com/releases/1998/02/980227055013.htm

13. How to Live it Now

1. http://richardwiseman.com/resources/The_Luck_Factor.pdf

Acknowledgments

I am so very grateful to the rock stars who helped bring this book to fruition: Author Coach Lisa Daily and my dear friend and editor, Simone Gers. Thank you to my wonderful co-author, Lee Savino, for always being willing to play in abundance mindset with me.

Thank you to the authors who were willing to share their stories for case studies and to all of you readers for joining me energetically on this journey to abundance.

I am also immeasurably grateful to the energetic coaches, teachers and healers I've had in my life, especially including Simone Gers, Erin Chanel, Katherine McIntosh, and the tools of Access Consciousness.®

About Renee Rose

15-time *USA Today* **bestselling romance author Renee Rose** is passionate about helping other authors find and maintain an abundance mindset to catapult their careers and create their best future. She employs energetic tools and techniques to help her clients clear resistance and money blocks, access their inner guidance, and tap into their love and appreciation for their books so they can achieve their dreams.

www.write2riches.com
renee@reneeroseromance.com

facebook.com/reneeroseromance

instagram.com/writetoriches

amazon.com/Renee-Rose/e/B008ASoFTo

bookbub.com/authors/renee-rose

tiktok.com/@write2riches

Made in the USA
Las Vegas, NV
03 December 2022